Sampler Stitchery

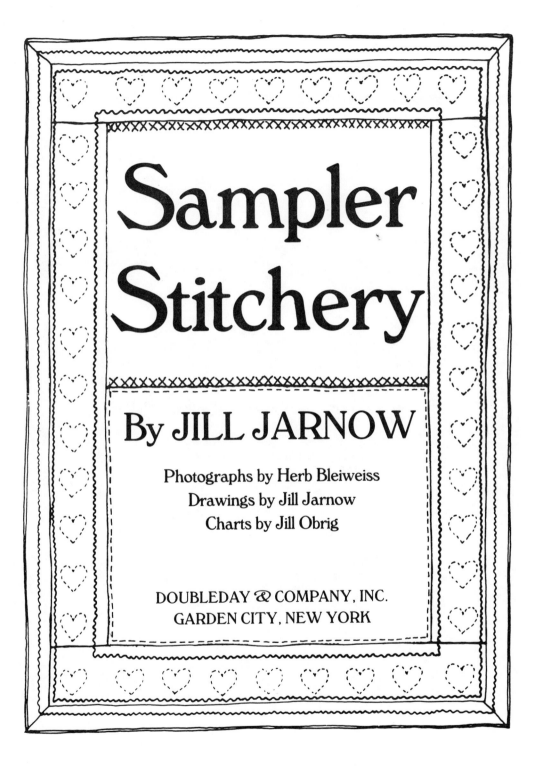

Sampler Stitchery

By JILL JARNOW

Photographs by Herb Bleiweiss
Drawings by Jill Jarnow
Charts by Jill Obrig

DOUBLEDAY & COMPANY, INC.
GARDEN CITY, NEW YORK

ISBN: 0-385-18531-6   AACR2
Library of Congress Catalog Card Number: 80–2415

COPYRIGHT © 1982 BY JILL JARNOW

Library of Congress Cataloging in Publication Data

Jarnow, Jill
   Sampler stitchery.

   Bibliography: p. 189
   1. Samplers. I. Title.
TT751.J37   746.3

9 8 7 6 5 4

Acknowledgments

Heartfelt thanks to my friends and family whose wonderful needlework is included in this book: the Aboffs, Dorothy Globus, Regina Larkin, Ann Lloyd, Betsy Potter, Vicki Rosenberg, and Connie Washburne.

More heartfelt thanks to Herb Bleiweiss and Rachel Newman, for their irreplaceable photography; to Jill Obrig, for her tireless charting and last-minute photographing of the Yellow Cat Pillow, Stencil Birthday Pillow, Stencil Alphabet Pillow, and Grandma Pillow; to Herb and Winnie Aboff, for the use of their special home as a photography location; to Cathy Knapp and the women at The Four Wives in Cold Spring Harbor, New York, for their generous advice; and to Marlene Connor, editor, for her wisdom, patience, and humor.

In Memory of Joan Aboff

Contents

Introduction

YESTERDAY'S SAMPLERS

The word *sampler* comes from the Latin word *exemplar* and is defined in the dictionary as "a pattern of work, an example." Early needlework samplers were, in fact, purely utilitarian. They were made to serve as stitch reference guides for repairing and marking household linen because pattern books were so scarce. As a result, stitchery samplers were well used. Rare, early samplers are on display in museums around the world.

The history of samplers in the United States dates back to the country's beginnings. Proficient mothers handed samplers down to their daughters, who were expected to stitch samplers of their own. They were time-consuming projects, and young girls began to sign and date their work.

Although samplers have taken a variety of forms, the image of the sampler we think of most often is rectangular in shape, containing an alphabet, name, date, and decorative designs. Such samplers were stitched in a combination of thread count (or cross-stitch) and decorative embroidery. Nineteenth-century girls in academies across the country were instructed to copy the letters and motifs from pattern books. Some drew their own designs, using existing prints or artwork for reference, with the help of a teacher. Then, using her chart, the needleworker embroidered regular cross-stitches into the fabric by counting the threads of the background material, even-weave linen with about 30 threads per inch. Although it was slow work, sampler making was considered an important part of a young girl's moral training.

Learning the alphabet was worthwhile, but having the endurance to complete a task had its own special value. Sometimes whimsical, often serious or self-righteous, yesterday's samplers have become important records of past people, places, and life-styles.

TODAY'S SAMPLERS

Children were the main sampler makers of yesteryear. Today, however, children have become involved with sports, television, and electronic games, leaving adults to carry on the sampler tradition. After a hectic day loaded with responsibilities, many adults find there is nothing so pleasurable as spending quiet, contemplative hours at work on stitchery.

The art of sampler making has evolved with the times. Although it is possible to copy the intricate samplers of yesterday, most people incorporate the qualities found in samplers they see in museums, historic societies, books, and magazines with today's needlework trends, creating informal, contemporary stitchery. With the exciting selection of fabric, thread, and reference materials now available, today's needleworker can find a greater range for self-expression than that enjoyed by our ancestors.

Today sampler stitchery can be interpreted in a variety of creative ways. The traditional sampler has found new flexibility. Whether in a cross-stitch motif used to decorate a baby sweater, cross-stitch letters personalizing a patchwork tote, or even the very contemporary use of stencil letters on pillows, the sampler influence will be unmistakable.

Because samplers and sampler-inspired items are so satisfying to work on, sampler stitchery, no matter what the interpretation, can be addictive. With one sampler complete, you often continue creating samplers or sampler-inspired gifts for family and friends, and these gifts will have a special place in any family for years to come.

THE QUEST FOR PERFECTION

The sampler projects in this book have inherited or borrowed qualities from their ancestors. But whether such qualities be the use of the alphabet, primitive symmetrical images, or moral instruction (of questionable value), the personal quality always dominates. Old samplers were, for the most part, stitched by young girls of varying degrees of skill. The imperfections and irregularities contribute as much to the charm of the needlework as does the precision. Remember this when making a sampler of your own, especially if you are new at stitchery. Be as neat and methodical as you can, but be realistic. While your stitches should not be so messy as to overwhelm the image, the quest for perfection should not inhibit you from creating an otherwise warm, personal, important piece of needlework.

GETTING STARTED

Choose a sampler project from this book according to your tastes and stitchery skills. If you are a beginner longing to create an intricate sampler to record an important event, such as the Hardanger Baby Sampler on page 62, start with an easier project that gives comparatively fast results, such as the Family Sampler on page 66. Slowly work your way up to the more demanding projects to avoid becoming overwhelmed.

Experienced needleworkers will be delighted to discover how stitchery procedures overlap from technique to technique. In many cases, the terms and materials are different but the stitches themselves are the same. You may feel awkward when you switch from needlepoint to counted-thread embroidery, for example, because the materials and tools are so different in size. But the awkwardness will last for only a short while.

UNDERSTANDING THE TERMS

Embroidery is a flexible term that encompasses all kinds of decorative stitchery on fabric. Cross-stitch, one of the myriad forms of embroidery, has many facets of its own. Counted-thread embroidery is the technique of placing cross-stitches according to the threads of fabric. For this, even-weave linen is easiest to use. Cross-stitching can also be done on plain fabric, or on fabric with threads too fine to count, with the aid of waste scrim or penelope mesh, which is basted in position over the fabric and removed when the stitching is complete. Gingham, with a large, clearly defined grid, is an ideal backing fabric for quick, informal cross-stitch projects, especially for beginners.

Needlepoint, done on mesh or canvas, was once more popularly known as canvas embroidery. Counted-thread embroidery and needlepoint are similar in stitch technique, so it is easy to switch back and forth between them if you remember that there are important basic differences. Counted-thread embroidery forms a pattern on the surface of the fabric, but much of the fabric remains visible when the stitching is complete. The exposed background is an important part of the design. Needlepoint is worked on canvas so that the stitches completely cover the backing material. A finished piece of needlepoint is much bulkier and stronger than a finished piece of counted-thread embroidery although each technique has its own special beauty and uses.

DECORATING WITH SAMPLERS

Use your finished sampler to enrich your environment or that of a friend or relative. Many of the projects in this collection make great wall hangings, but you may want to consider other sampler-inspired items, such as pillows, rugs, bedspreads, handbags, and clothing decoration.

Sampler stitchery blends well with all types of decor from a room full of antiques to a contemporary space. Samplers are as appropriate in rooms for adults as they are in rooms for children. But be sure to choose materials and stitch techniques that are geared to the job you have in mind. Cross-stitch done on gingham, the fastest of the techniques, works beautifully on pillows, bedspreads, and clothing accessories. Durable and charming, cross-stitch on gingham is distinctly informal. Needlepoint, the strongest of the hand embroideries, is perfect for rugs, pillows, and belts but would be impractical for a baby bib or bedcover. Delicate counted-thread embroidery is durable enough for pillows, clothing decoration, or linens, but would not last long if used on the floor. Both needlepoint and counted-thread embroidery will be as formal or informal as the image you choose to stitch.

For specifics on materials, stitch techniques, and display procedures, see the following sections.

Sampler Stitchery

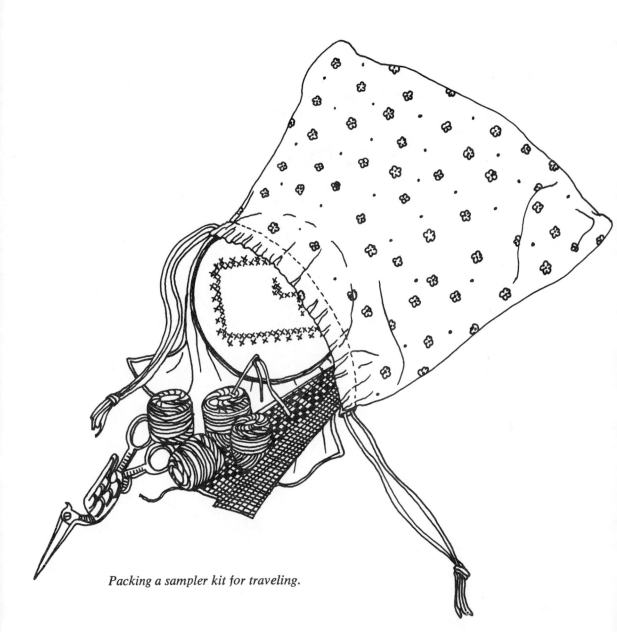

Packing a sampler kit for traveling.

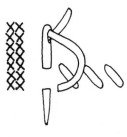

Work Habits

THE PORTABLE SAMPLER

A sampler project needs very little special equipment and can travel with you wherever you go. Whether you choose the formal Hardanger Baby Sampler on page 62 or the whimsical Sampler Birthday Pillow on page 117, you can stitch everywhere: as you ride to work, on a lunch or afternoon break, relaxing at home during the evening, or on vacation. Even the Gingham Sampler Quilt on page 129, which is quite large when finished, can be stitched square by square while you're on the go and assembled later when all the squares are complete.

ASSEMBLING A PERSONAL SAMPLER KIT

Here's what you'll need for your own personal sampler kit:

1. A chart of the design (from this book or another source), with an additional graph paper chart, if needed, containing your own specific information.
2. Appropriate fabric.
3. Thread or yarn.
4. Needle.
5. Small, sharp scissors.
6. Embroidery hoop, where needed.
7. Carrying bag.

Work anywhere! Sampler stitchery travels beautifully because most projects are so easy to pack and unpack. But be sure to keep your fabric and thread clean by storing them in a bag or basket between stitching sessions. For storage, tack the needle through the fabric, but prevent possible rust stains by placing the needle near an outside edge, well away from the area to be stitched.

If you find yourself working at a dining table on a lunch break, take special care that your needlework doesn't become stained with insidious crumbs of food or nasty spots. In fact, always remember to wipe any surface before you pull out your materials to begin work.

LIGHTING

Although you can work on most projects during the day, using available light, some of the finer linens are hard to see and will require the best possible lighting conditions. While full sun is usually too bright, indirect natural light is ideal.

At night or in a dark room during the day, lamplight is fine, although finding a satisfactory seating/lighting arrangement can be difficult. Either a table-clamped gooseneck or a free-standing pharmacy-style lamp is a worthwhile investment if you are an active needleworker with a lighting problem; both are easy to adjust.

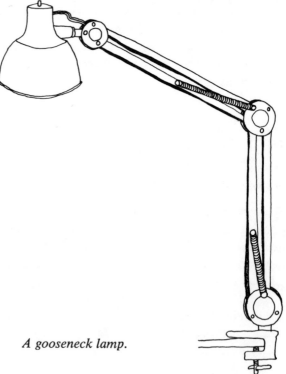

A gooseneck lamp.

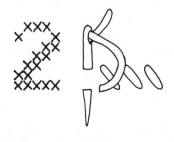

Materials

WHERE TO SHOP, HOW TO SHOP

Buy good-quality supplies at needlework specialty shops or department stores in your area. Find them by looking under "Needlework" or "Art Needlework" in your local telephone Yellow Pages. Most often, needlework supplies are priced fairly and shops with better-quality supplies are more expensive. However, if you have several shops to choose from, consider comparing prices and quality before making large purchases. The personal service you receive in a small shop, such as help with color coordinating and stitchery instruction, is sometimes reflected in the cost of the materials. Since this guidance can be very helpful to you, it is often worth the extra expense.

Whenever possible, shop in person because the materials, threads, and yarns you choose will greatly affect the look of your finished needlework. Although standard fabrics such as hardanger, Aida cloth, or needlepoint mesh are easy to order by mail, linen for embroidery defies exact description, particularly when you must choose between subtle colors such as "natural" and "off-white."

Some of the projects in this book are described with specific brand and color notations to help you purchase supplies locally or order them by mail from the sources listed in the following pages. You may, however, want to make color changes in these projects according to your own tastes and decorating needs. This will be difficult to do by mail unless you have a piece of fabric, wallpaper, or other swatch to use for reference and you can locate a mail-order source willing to work with you. When corresponding with a supplier, be as specific as possible and always remember that color choice is a matter of personal taste. Since you will be dependent upon the salesperson to make decisions, you can't always be sure of what you will receive. You may like what arrives, or you may not. For more on adapting colors, see page 20.

MAIL-ORDER SOURCES

Boutique Margot: 26 West Fifty-fourth Street, New York, N.Y. 10019. This shop specializes in cross-stitch supplies and books.

The Counting House: P.O. Box 155, Pawleys Island, S.C. 29585. This shop has a full line of pattern books and cross-stitch supplies.

The Four Wives: 43 Main Street, Cold Spring Harbor, N.Y. Although it specializes in needlepoint supplies, this shop also carries embroidery materials.

Handcraft from Europe: P.O. Box 372, Sausalito, Calif. 94965. Check this shop for a wide range of needlework materials.

Needle Nuts, Inc.: 532 Elm Street, Houston, Tex. 77081. A distributor of Paternayan yarns, excellent for needlepoint.

THE IMPORTANCE OF GOOD-QUALITY MATERIALS

Sampler making implies longevity and tradition. More than any other form of needlework, samplers are treasured, displayed, and passed on to the next generation of the family. Keep this sense of tradition in mind when you decide on your design and when you purchase or collect materials; choose only the best available.

SCRAPS FOR SAMPLERS

Scraps or leftover materials are appropriate for samplers if you choose them with care. When selecting leftovers from stitchery projects, exercise the same discretion as if you were purchasing new material. Even if you have no scraps now, when you complete your first sampler project you will undoubtedly have threads and fabric left over. Store these away carefully. They are the beginning of an important stockpile.

BUYING MATERIALS

If you purchase materials for your sampler, buy only clean, undamaged ones. You will be spending hours on your stitchery, so use materials that are worth the time you expend. They will repay you by remaining fresh and beautiful.

Whenever possible, buy fabrics, threads, and yarns of natural fibers. One hundred percent cotton or wool products are more expensive than their synthetic counterparts and are often hard to find. They have many important advantages, however, and are well worth the extra cost and effort.

Most important is the beauty of the material. Needlework done in cotton, wool, or silk thread has a special surface sheen not usually attainable with acrylic or polyester. Although I have read of high-quality synthetic thread imported from Europe, I have not yet seen it.

Synthetic embroidery fabrics and those made with a high percentage of acrylic are usually not as beautiful as those of cotton or linen. But even more distressing is their tendency to pill and stain. Inexpensive synthetics cannot even endure the long-term handling necessary to complete a sampler, becoming worn and battered before they are finished.

Aside from aesthetics, good-quality yarns and fabrics are much easier to use than less expensive acrylics. Synthetic wool and needlepoint mesh are so prone to knotting and snagging that they will frustrate you as you work, taking a great deal of pleasure out of the process. As with other synthetics, these materials soon become limp and shabby.

Unfortunately, certain fabrics such as gingham are, at this writing, practically impossible to find in cotton or in a high-percentage-cotton blend. In order to make the Sampler Baby Bib (page 144), the Gingham Sampler Quilt (page 129), or the Sampler Birthday Pillow (page 117), you will have to use cotton-blend gingham or, worse, 100 percent polyester. Perhaps you have cotton gingham stored away in a scrap bag or live near a store that still carries an old stock of cotton!

CHOOSING THE RIGHT EVEN-WEAVE FABRIC FOR CROSS-STITCH

As the number of threads per inch of fabric increases, the more intricate the stitchery will need to be. Aida cloth with 8 threads to the inch is easier and faster to stitch than hardanger with 22 threads per inch. Although linen with 36 threads to the inch requires no special skills, completing a sampler with tiny stitches can be painstaking. It is a challenge I recommend for experienced needleworkers.

Whether you choose to copy a project from this book or are designing a sampler of your own, select fabric that matches your skills and interests. If you are new at cross-stitching, don't overwhelm yourself with a first project that is too demanding. Consider beginning with one of the larger-mesh projects, such as the Family Sampler on page 66 or the Sampler Birthday Pillow on page 117. Once you complete a quick cross-stitch project you will be ready for slower, more time-consuming stitchery.

Pair any cross-stitch sampler chart given in this book with any fabric that catches your eye, but choose material with care. The size of the finished sampler and the patience needed to complete it will depend on the thread count of the fabric. A sampler worked on finely woven fabric will be smaller than the same sampler design worked on a large, bulky-mesh background. Each will have its own distinct character.

THE TRUTH ABOUT EVEN-WEAVE FABRIC

Although fabric described as "even-weave" is popular for counted-thread embroidery, neatly woven fabrics such as hardanger or Aida are sometimes not as perfect as they appear. As you count the threads of hardanger in preparation for stitching, you may discover the fabric has 23 threads per inch along one direction instead of the usual 22. While this will prevent your stitching from being exact, the slight irregularity can add flavor and charm to your needlework.

Contemporary sampler makers tend to advocate the use of this so-called even-weave fabric to the exclusion of all else. I feel this is a mistake. If you can see the threads of a fabric well enough to count them, consider it for cross-stitch. Our ancestors didn't have much of a variety from which to choose. When one looks at historic samplers it is evident that nothing was rejected because the threads were slightly irregular.

When you use fabric with a different thread count in each direction, the cross-stitches you make will not be square. If the threads themselves are of irregular thickness, this, too, will cause your stitches to be uneven. The Dish Towel Sampler on page 91 is stitched on linen toweling with doubled, uneven vertical threads. When I cross-stitched the alphabet, I treated each doubled thread as one. The resulting alphabet is short and wide, with a charming antique look. For a more uniform contemporary feeling, or for easier stitching, choose an even-weave fabric with a large, clear structure, such as those mentioned above.

HOW MUCH TO BUY

To determine the amount of fabric you will need for a specific project, count the number of stitches in both the horizontal and vertical axes of the charted design. Purchase fabric that has the same number of threads as you have counted, plus an additional 2 to 4 inches on each side for seam allowance, hemming, and other finishing procedures. Make all personal adjustments to a charted design to establish any size change from the chart shown before purchasing fabric. (See Chapter Three, "Personalizing Your Samplers.")

If you shop in a good-quality needlework store, an experienced salesperson should be able to help you with yarn or thread amounts for specific projects. Keep the unused yarn neat and clean. Large amounts of leftovers are often exchangeable, but check with the shopkeeper at the time of the purchase.

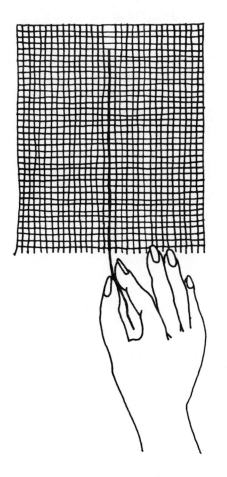

Pulling a thread.

TRIMMING LINEN

When you purchase linen for needlework from a reputable supply shop, the salesperson will pull a thread of the linen across the entire width of the fabric as a guide for cutting. This precaution, although time-consuming, will ensure that you get a perfectly squared piece of fabric. Use the same technique at home when trimming fabric to prevent your material from becoming unusably crooked. You can lose up to 3 inches of expensive fabric when you cut incorrectly by eye.

FABRIC TYPES

Canvas for Needlepoint

Needlepoint canvas is an open-mesh material that has been stiffened with sizing. The most popular type, made with evenly spaced holes, is constructed with either single (mono) threads or, in the stronger "interlock" version, with pairs of threads twisted around each other as they were woven. Interlock canvas with 5 squares to the inch is used for quick-point rug stitching.

Penelope, or double-thread canvas, is also woven from pairs of threads, but the overall structure of the mesh is evenly spaced holes that are alternately large and small in each direction.

Needlepoint canvas is available in a variety of sizes and materials. Wherever possible, use the best-quality cotton canvas for the project you are doing.

Fabric for Embroidery

The following fabrics are made abroad especially for counted-thread stitchery and are available in various-sized weaves and colors. Stitchery done on these materials will have a neat, even appearance.

Aida Cloth

Woven cotton threads are drawn together in groups of four to form small, easily visible squares, 8 to the inch. It is available in white, natural, and beige.

Pearl Aida, a smaller version, has 10 to 12 squares to the inch. You may find Pearl Aida in bright colors such as blue or yellow, but the thread count may be different along each axis, so be sure to account for this when planning your project.

Binca cloth is a coarse version of Aida cloth.

Hardanger Cloth

Hardanger, sometimes called monk's cloth, is usually available with 22 threads per inch, although traditional Norwegian hardanger embroidery has been done on fabric as fine as 50 threads per inch. Coarser-meshed hardanger-style fabrics are available at needlework specialty stores in a range of colors.

Material for Cross-stitch

Needlepoint Canvas

Although it's not a favorite of contemporary needleworkers, penelope needlepoint canvas was occasionally used for cross-stitch in the nineteenth century as if it were fine linen. The 1831 Sampler shown on page 83, with the foreground stitched and the threads of the background mesh left uncovered, is an example of this historic stitchery. You can easily copy this technique, but be sure to keep track of all the ends of thread. In addition to the stitches on the front, every stitch you take on the back will be visible, too!

Linen

Many historic samplers combine counted-thread cross-stitch and other forms of embroidery on very fine linen with approximately 30 to 40 threads per inch. To create a sampler with an antique appearance, use threads in muted colors and choose a small-weave linen. The even-weave fabrics previously described are generally too coarse for anything but the most geometric embroidery stitches. Linen, usually imported from Switzerland, France, or Scandinavia, is available in 14 to 36 threads per inch in white, ecru, beige, and an assortment of colors. Counted-thread embroidery done on linen will have an irregular historic look.

Scrim

To cross-stitch on linen with threads too fine to count, use scrim, a double-thread canvas similar to penelope but lighter-weight, and available in 7 to 15 meshes to the inch. Discard it when your cross-stitching is complete, as described on page 81.

If you have trouble finding scrim in your local needlework shop, order it from one of the cross-stitch specialty stores listed on page 4.

Gingham

Choose gingham fabric for simple, fast cross-stitching; it is ideal for beginners and children. Gingham is woven with a checked pattern and is available at fabric stores in a variety of sizes—8 boxes (or checks) per inch is a good basic choice. For more on gingham, see page 23.

For extra body and easier stitching, first baste lightweight muslin or white cotton fabric to the back of the gingham. When working, place cross-stitches within the boxes, being careful to insert the needle into the corners.

THREAD

Always experiment before beginning a new project to make sure thread, material, and stitch sizes are well suited. Thread that is too heavy or stitches that are too large will overwhelm the fabric. Stitches or threads that are too delicate will be lost. Finding the best combinations can often be a trial-and-error procedure.

Special note: I have indicated, wherever possible, brand names, colors, and amounts needed for projects in this book. Use the following information when you choose threads and wool for your own designs or improvisations.

Six-strand Embroidery Floss (Mouliné Spécial)

This is the most common cotton embroidery thread. It is composed of six tiny strands of two-ply cotton, which you can use in their entirety or separate into smaller groupings for delicate stitching.

To avoid snarling when separating threads, cut the floss 18 to 20 inches long, a comfortable length for stitching. Next separate the strands by rolling them between your thumb and forefinger. Gently draw out the number of strands needed and store away the remainder for later use, perhaps for combining with other leftovers.

DMC floss, available in needlework shops and department stores, comes in a wide range of beautiful subtle colors. Coats & Clark makes a less expensive six-strand floss that is sold in variety and fabric shops. Although many of the colors are attractive, choose with care, as some tend to be unpleasantly garish. Both brands are packaged in small pull skeins.

Pearl Cotton (Coton Perlé)

DMC also makes pearl cotton, an elegant embroidery floss that comes in one long continuous, twisted two-ply strand. The twist will give your stitching a pearly surface. This floss is available in balls and skeins; the balls are easier to use, as the skeins must be completely taken apart. Pearl cotton is manufactured in four weights: 3, 5, 8, and 12. Size 3 is the heaviest. For delicate work, choose size 8 or 12 rather than try to separate strands. The projects in this book use sizes 5 and 8.

DMC pearl cotton is not available in the same range of colors as the DMC floss, which can be frustrating when you are planning a project. However, you can successfully use pearl cotton next to six-strand floss for an interesting textural effect.

Retors à Broder

Retors à Broder, available in better needlework stores, is a bulky, single-strand, five-ply cotton thread made by DMC that comes in a wide variety of matte colors. Strong and durable, it is heavier than ✕3 pearl cotton and combines well with Aida cloth (see page 8).

YARN

Persian Yarn

Persian yarn is best for needlepoint. Made of long-fibered virgin wool, it is known for its good canvas coverage, luster, and durability.

Although there are many brands on the market, my favorite is Paternayan, available in several hundred colors at good needlework shops around the country. Several of the needlepoint projects described in this book are given with specific Paternayan color numbers, which you may find useful if you have a Paternayan dealer in your area or when you order yarn through the mail. Other companies do make good Persian yarns, and if these are more readily available, you may wish to use them. Colors are often surprisingly different from brand to brand, so you may feel more confident buying yarns in person rather than through the mail.

Persian wool is available in 1-ounce skeins or in precut lengths. Most shops will break a 1-ounce skein into a smaller amount. Don't be afraid to buy a large quantity in one dye lot for use in a background, as many shops will take exchanges on unused portions. Of course, be sure to ask at the time of the purchase.

Persian yarn is also available in smaller, prepackaged amounts, measured by the yard, sold at department stores and elsewhere. The color range and general quality are, however, usually not as good as Persian wool sold by the ounce.

Each length of Persian yarn is composed of three individual strands of two-ply wool. The number of strands you need will depend on the size of the mesh you are using, as shown on the chart on the following page. Separate one strand from a group of three by pulling it away with an upward motion. Make thicker combinations of yarn by adding strands as needed. When beginning an original project, experiment to be sure the yarn completely covers the needlepoint canvas. Even with the projects described in this book, occasionally one color of yarn will be thinner or thicker than usual and you will have to adjust the number of strands you use. When you are covering a large background area with dark wool, you may consider covering the mesh with an acrylic wash before beginning to stitch, as described on page 105.

Tapestry Yarn

Tapestry yarn is also available for needlepoint. It is sold in department stores in 40-yard skeins and pull skeins, both composed of four-ply wool twisted into a single strand. The color range is wide, and the dye lots of the DMC brand tapestry yarn, in particular, are remarkably consistent. To cover 10- and 12-thread-to-the-inch canvas, use the continental stitch with a single strand of tapestry yarn in your needle. Tapestry yarn is smoother than Persian, and needlepoint worked with tapestry yarn will not have the same silky surface sheen.

SELECTING THREAD AND YARN WEIGHTS

Select thread and yarn sizes for samplers in this book according to the information given for each project. When you make your own adaptations (combining a chart with your own fabric selection), use common sense when choosing yarn or thread. A salesperson in a needlework shop may make valuable suggestions, but if you are in doubt do a sample swatch to determine what weight thread is best. Your stitches should be visible on the fabric but not too bulky.

Here is basic information for determining thread weights, but since brands and dye lots differ, especially with Persian yarns, be sure to make any adjustments as they seem necessary. There are many more types of thread, yarn, and fabric than those mentioned below, so be sure to experiment when you find materials you like.

GUIDE FOR CHOOSING MATERIALS

FOR COUNTED-THREAD EMBROIDERY

Fabric type	Recommended thread size
Hardanger cloth with 22 threads per inch	⅜8 pearl cotton or 3 strands of embroidery floss
Aida cloth with 8 squares per inch	⅜8 pearl cotton or 3 strands of embroidery floss
Pearl Aida cloth with 10–12 squares per inch	⅜5 pearl cotton or 6 strands of embroidery floss
Gingham with 8 squares per inch	⅜8 pearl cotton or 3 strands of embroidery floss

FOR NEEDLEPOINT

Canvas size	Recommended yarn amounts
12–14 threads to the inch	2 strands of Persian yarn
10 threads to the inch	3 strands (or one full length) of Persian yarn
5 threads to the inch (quick point)	6–8 strands of Persian yarn

NEEDLES: EMBROIDERY AND TAPESTRY

Embroidery needles have long eyes to accommodate different thicknesses of embroidery thread or yarn. They are available in sizes 1–4, 5, 7, 9, and 11. Size 1 is the largest, size 11 the smallest.

Tapestry needles are larger than embroidery needles. They have blunt points that will slide easily through needlepoint or other open-weave mesh without puncturing you or the fabric. The eyes are wide and smooth inside to lessen the stress on the wool or thread as you stitch. They are available in sizes 13–26. Size 13 is the largest, size 26 the smallest.

HOOPS AND FRAMES

For neat, even embroidery stitches, use a hoop or frame to keep your fabric taut while you work. Although a frame isn't always necessary for needlepoint done with predominantly the basketweave stitch, it is useful for limiting canvas distortion when doing the continental stitch or decorative needlepoint.

Small, inexpensive hoops, available in variety and needlework stores, are appropriate for most of the embroidery projects in this book. Choose a hoop according to the size of the project. A hoop that is too small will slow you down as you work because you will have to stop continually to reposition the fabric. A hoop that is too big will not grip the fabric properly.

Larger, more expensive frames for needlepoint and embroidery are available in needlework supply shops.

ACCESSORIES

Useful accessories that will make your sampler experience more enjoyable include a small pair of sharp scissors with straight points for cutting thread and yarn; larger, sharp scissors for cutting fabric; a work basket for holding threads, charts, fabric, embroidery hoop, and needles; a tape measure or ruler; and a thimble.

If you plan to carry your sampler project with you, be sure to use an appropriately sized bag for protecting materials.

BUYING AND USING GRAPH PAPER

You will need graph paper, which is available in stationery and art supply stores, to complete most of the samplers shown in this book. It is convenient if you can match the size of the graph paper to the size of the fabric you are stitching. Most samplers are worked over 2 threads at a time, so graph paper with 10 boxes per inch will match fabric with 20 threads to the inch. But since this is rarely possible, think in terms of stitch count, not size correlations. Your name graphed on paper with 8 boxes to the inch will be much smaller than the actual stitching in the Quick Point Sampler Rug on page 103, which has a mesh of 5 threads to the inch. However, it will be much larger than the actual stitching in the Hardanger Baby Sampler on page 62, which is done on a much smaller mesh.

Be practical also. If your needlework project is large, such as the Needle-point Rug, it will be easier to do your charting on a moderate-size piece of paper. Even if you can find graph paper with the same 5 lines to the inch as the needlepoint mesh, it may be more convenient to work on and carry around a smaller piece of paper with a finer grid.

Samplers on small-meshed fabrics can also cause problems, since graph paper with very small boxes may be hard to locate. Alternatively, chart out the information on graph paper with larger boxes, but be prepared to use more than one sheet and piece them together with clear tape.

If the personal and place names you wish to stitch are shorter than those shown in the samplers in this book, you will be able to do your charting conveniently on almost any size of graph paper. (If the names are longer, you may have to piece sheets together.) However, to center your informa-tion, it will still be necessary to work with stitch counts, as described in the centering section on page 22.

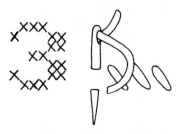

Personalizing Your Samplers

ALPHABETS

Use the alphabets that follow to personalize the sampler projects given in this book, or use the alphabets to create sampler designs of your own. See page 83 (the 1831 Sampler) for a script alphabet.

THE IMPORTANCE OF YOUR SIGNATURE

Embroidery styles differ from person to person, just as handwriting styles differ, but sampler stitchery brings yet another dimension of personality to your needlework. You may copy a design stitch for stitch from this book, but in the end you will include your own personal information and signature. If the idea of signing your needlework seems insignificant or even pretentious, compare the experiences of looking at a beautifully stitched unsigned sampler and looking at a beautiful signed and dated piece. Signed needlework is infinitely more charming and interesting.

Needlework identified by time, place, and person creates its own special history. Whether made one hundred years ago or finished yesterday, stitchery marked with personal identification will speak forever. Using an alphabet shown in this book, stitch your full name in a prominent location as part of the overall sampler design or add your initials unobtrusively in a corner. Even in the simplest form, your identity will have lasting importance.

16

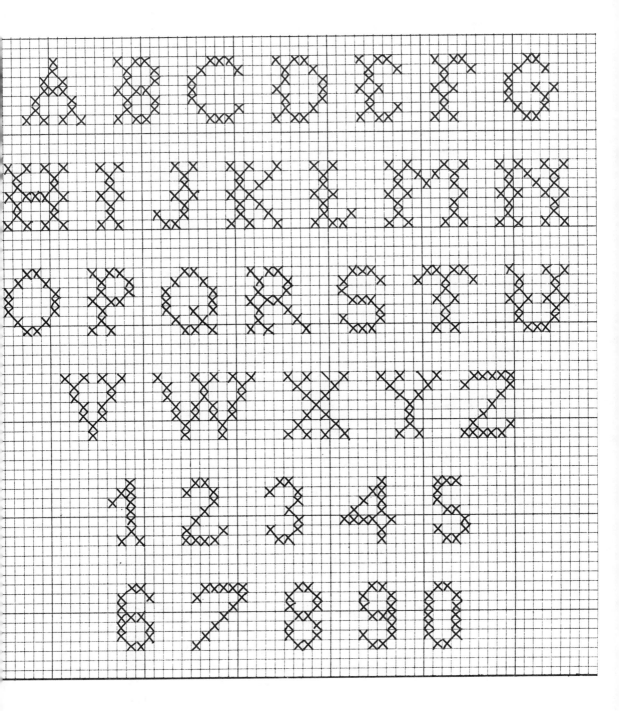

Traditional cross-stitch alphabet.

ADDING NAMES

When you choose projects from this book such as the Wise Old Owl Sampler on page 97 or the Hardanger Baby Sampler on page 62, you only need to add your name or initials in the appropriate place. Some projects, however, such as the Family Sampler on page 66 or the Sampler Tote on page 122, will need larger adjustments, according to the length of the names you use. Making these adaptations is simple and satisfying; specific instructions accompany the appropriate projects. The finished needlework will, of course, be slightly different in size and shape from the example shown, but this is an important, positive quality of personalization.

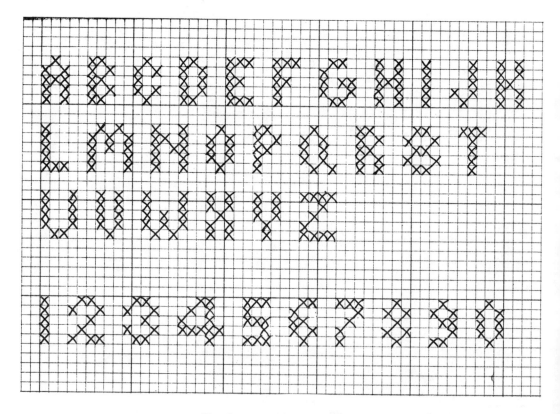

Simple cross-stitch alphabet.

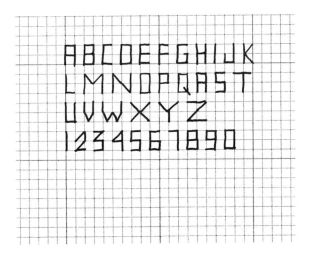

Backstitch alphabet.

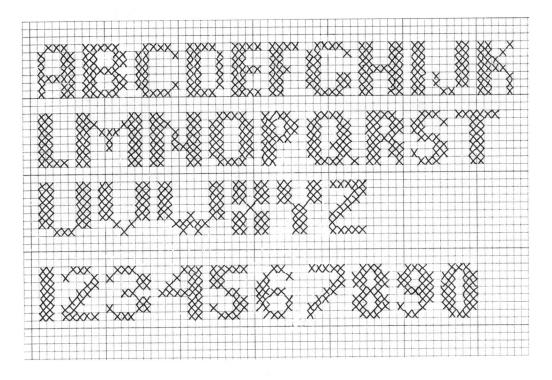

New York City Sampler alphabet.

COLOR CHANGES

Aside from adding your own information to a given sampler design, you may also want to change a few of the suggested colors so that the finished needlework is more pleasing to you. Perhaps you want to adjust the colors to coordinate with your bedroom or living room color scheme. Whatever the reason, reorganizing colors is easy and rewarding.

Take a swatch of fabric, wallpaper, a paint chip, a picture, or other color reference to your local needlework store. Use it as a guide for choosing new colors of thread. or wool. Salespersons in small, good-quality supply shops are usually willing and able to assist you, so don't be afraid to ask for help.

If you buy supplies through the mail, it will be harder to make color changes. See page 3 for more information.

CREATING PERSONAL SAMPLERS

Once you start altering the charts given in this book, you will soon want to create your own personal samplers from scratch. Plan your design on graph paper first by combining all your favorite images, borders, and alphabets. Use the information given here to help you choose materials, design motifs, and do your stitchery. Let the charted samplers be inspiration, but also check through books listed in the Bibliography, which are available in libraries and bookstores.

For invaluable inspiration, visit museums and local preservation societies to see historic stitchery at first hand. Some museums may even have slides of their samplers that you can buy, rent, or borrow. These will give you a chance to see an enlarged view of stitch patterns.

If you find yourself becoming a sampler fanatic, keep a notebook and clipping file for permanent reference. Graph paper notebooks are available in stationery and art supply stores.

PREPARING WORDS FOR CENTERING

To add your name, location, or the date to any sampler chart given in this book, mark out the letters and figures on graph paper, using the alphabet suggested for each project. Specifics on spacing are described later in this chapter. Separate the material you graph according to how it will be stitched in the sampler.

To center a line, count the number of boxes or stitches charted on paper from the beginning to the end of a line, including all spaces between letters and words. Mark on your chart the center line or center box of the characters to be stitched.

If you are charting more than one row of words and figures to be stitched in consecutive, parallel rows, also count the number of spaces in the height, including the spaces above, below, and in between the lines. Mark the center lines on both your graph and the chart in the book. Stitch long basting lines to mark the horizontal and vertical centers of the fabric to be stitched, as described on the following pages. Using the basting lines as a guide, begin stitching in the center of each line of letters, as described in the following sections.

ENLARGING SAMPLERS

If your lettering is too long to fit into the space shown for any sampler in this book, consider using letter or number abbreviations where appropriate. Information for enlarging samplers is given under specific projects, but you may adapt any sampler on a piece of graph paper by adding extra rows to the width and length of an existing chart. When you are planning to lengthen a repeat border, especially one that turns corners, add stitches to the center of each side to preserve the corner patterns and keep the border sides symmetrical. For more, see page 24.

LETTER AND WORD SPACING

Because each letter of the alphabet is a different size and shape, there is no exact rule for spacing. However, here are suggestions to help you learn to space your letters and words gracefully.

Leave at least one thread blank between every letter or line of letters that you stitch. Leave 4 to 6 threads blank between words.

Close-fitting letters, words, and lines are more satisfying to read than those that are stretched out, but lettering that is too tightly spaced is illegible. Learn what spacing is best by trial and error. Each alphabet will have different requirements, so until you are experienced, be prepared to remove and restitch words that look wrong. Consistency and visual impact are important, but be realistic. Small imperfections in word spacing can contribute to the charm of a piece of needlework if they are not blatant.

CENTERING ON EVEN-WEAVE FABRIC

Chart on graph paper the letters and figures necessary for personalizing your sampler project, as described above.

To center a design on even-weave fabric, determine the total width and length of the design by counting the threads of the fabric. The stitch count of the area to be stitched should be the same across the width and down the length of the fabric as the stitch count found on the graphed design. Mark the outside boundaries of the design with basting stitches, always positioning the selvage edge of the fabric to the left.

Be sure to leave extra rows of fabric beyond the borders of the stitching on all sides for seam allowance. For needlepoint, 2 to 4 inches is advisable, the more the better if you plan to do your own blocking and mounting. For embroidery, 2 inches will be adequate.

Once the outside basting lines are in position, count the threads between them again and run a basting line down the center of the fabric. Count the threads between the top and bottom basting lines and add a basting line across the center of the fabric. Find and mark the horizontal and vertical centers on both the graphed design shown in this book and the graph containing your own lettering. Begin your stitchery in the center of the design

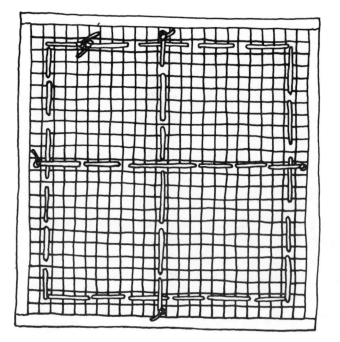

BASTING LINES.

Count the threads and use basting lines to mark the edges and center axes of the sampler.

Bind the edges of the fabric with masking tape or hand stitching.

by first placing the stitches that are nearest the vertical and horizontal axes. Work back and forth, matching the stitch placement on the fabric to the stitches in the graphs. Remove the basting lines by cutting away small areas as they interfere with your stitching.

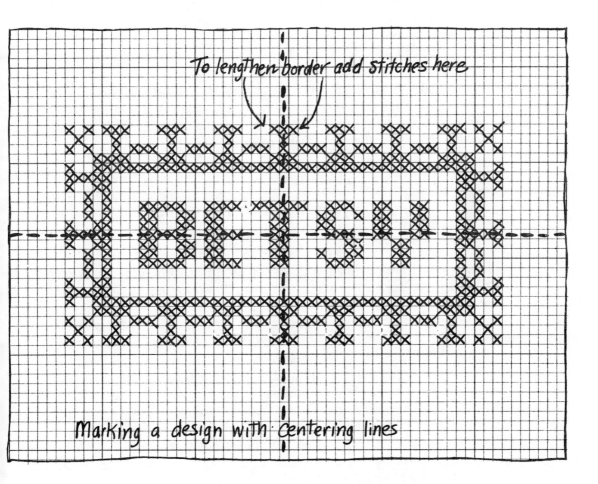

CENTERING ON GINGHAM

To center a design on gingham, fold the fabric in half lengthwise and place a basting stitch in the crease, along the edge of the gingham boxes indicated by the fold.

Open the fabric and fold in the opposite direction. Baste through the creased fold as it runs along the edge of the gingham boxes.

Open the fabric and press flat. There should be no folds or creases remaining, only two lines of basting.

BORDER AND CORNER DESIGNS

Border designs with repeat patterns are important elements in both historic and contemporary samplers. The border designs of historic samplers tend to have nonsymmetrical corners. The design travels neatly around the outside edges of the sampler without regard for whether the corners match. Contemporary sampler makers seem to be more concerned with symmetry. Today's samplers almost always have neatly matching corners.

When adapting a sampler graphed in this collection, you will have to deal with the same issue of corners. If you want to keep the corners matching as shown (or make them symmetrical where they are not) while enlarging or reducing a design for your own needs, be sure to add stitches to the center of each side of the border as shown in the drawing on page 23. If you are not bothered by informal borders, more power to you!

CORNERING BORDERS

If you are designing your own sampler and want to include symmetrical corners, you will have to plan your corner design first on graph paper and work the rest of your border design into this. To work out neat corners, use an inexpensive mirror that can reflect right down to the edge.

Graph out a short length of your border. Place the edge of the mirror along the graphed border at a 45-degree angle. Move the mirror up and down the border until you find a spot where it makes a perfect right angle in the border without cutting any motifs in half and without leaving too much space in between the stitches. Use the mirror as a straightedge to trace the line of the 45-degree angle right onto the graph. Remove the mirror, and copy the mirror image (the reversed image) of the border onto the empty side of the drawn line. Work from the corner out to create a neat, even corner design. Use this design in the remaining three corners, adjusting the connecting border motifs as necessary.

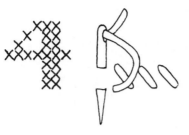

Techniques

USING CHARTS

Graphed charts are provided to enable you to reproduce the needlework projects shown in this book. These charted designs, or those from any other source, may be interpreted in either cross-stitch or needlepoint. Unless otherwise specified, each square on the graph equals one cross-stitch made over 2 threads of linen. For cross-stitch on gingham, the marks on the chart match the gingham square for square, although the size of the graph and gingham boxes may differ. For needlepoint, each graphed box indicates one standard continental stitch. When using a cross-stitch chart to create needlepoint, you will have to provide background stitches that are not shown in the chart in order to complete your needlework; background color recommendations are, however, not given.

The stitch colors are indicated by letter or pictorial symbols and are explained in a key accompanying each chart.

Satin stitch, backstitch, french knots, and other embroidery stitches—when used in combination with cross-stitch or continental stitch—are indicated in the appropriate places, usually with separate charts of their own.

For more stitch information, see Chapter Five, "Stitches." For specifics on choosing materials, see Chapter Two, "Materials," or the information given for the project you have chosen.

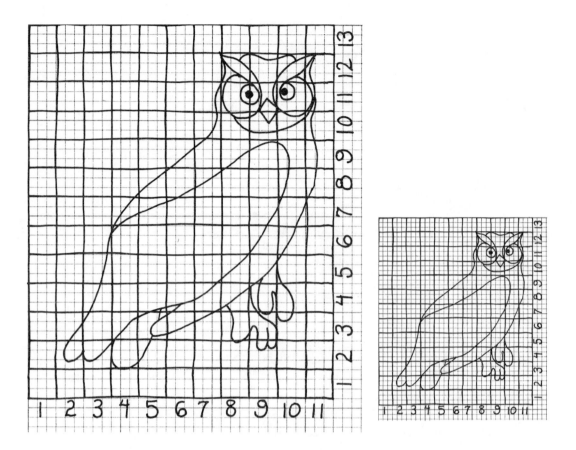

Enlarging or reducing art using grids.

ENLARGING A DESIGN FOR EMBROIDERY

To enlarge artwork to embroider from this book or any other source, use corresponding grids. First trace the original artwork onto translucent, unlined paper such as tracing paper, vellum, or layout bond paper. Use a ruler and pencil to draw a grid of equal-sized squares directly over the artwork. Number the boxes across the top and down the side. (Or transfer artwork directly to graph paper using a sunny window or light table, as described in the next section, to enable you to see through the paper.)

Next draw a larger grid with larger squares on another piece of paper, the size you want your sampler to be. Use graph paper to make the job easier. Be sure the new grid contains the same number of squares as the original and is numbered in the same way. If you want your enlarged drawings to match specific measurements, such as the 1¾-inch squares of the Dish Towel Sampler on page 91, make the sides of each enlargement square 1¾ inches (or the size desired) and divide them into equal segments.

Note where each line of the artwork being enlarged crosses the smaller grid; put a dot at the corresponding place on the larger grid. When all of the dots are marked, connect them to complete the enlargement.

To reduce a design, reverse the procedure: make a grid of squares smaller than the original and mark off the artwork, square by square, as described above.

TRANSFERRING A DESIGN FOR EMBROIDERY

Although most sampler designs can be copied by following charts given in this book or from other sources, some samplers, such as the Wise Old Owl Sampler on page 97, contain pictorial embroidery, in which the threads are not counted, as well as cross-stitch. When you transfer the artwork to fabric, as described below, be sure to leave enough room for the cross-stitch embroidery and finishing procedures. For best results, count threads carefully as you work.

To transfer a design to fabric for embroidery, first trace it onto transparent paper, such as tracing paper or layout paper, available in stationery and art supply stores.

Always work on a flat, hard, clean surface. Iron out any wrinkles in the fabric and lay the ironed fabric face up on the work surface. Smooth out bulges with the side of your hand and secure the material in place with masking tape. Place the artwork face up over the fabric and tape securely down one side. Place dressmaker's carbon paper face down between the artwork and the fabric. Choose a color that will be visible on the embroidery fabric. Pressing firmly, carefully trace around the design, using a hard pencil.

If the placement of the design is critical, transfer the artwork to the fabric against a sunny window or artist's light table. Tape the artwork face up on the window. Position the fabric over it, face up, and tape securely. Trace the design with a sharp, hard pencil.

TRANSFERRING A DESIGN FOR NEEDLEPOINT

Although all needlepoint projects in this book are accompanied by charts, at some point you may want to transfer a design to needlepoint mesh for stitchery. Enlarge the artwork as previously described and darken the outlines. Tape the artwork, face up, on a hard surface and then tape the mesh in place over it. Trace the artwork onto the mesh with a waterproof marker or acrylic paint. Double-check that all markers are waterproof before using by drawing on a piece of fabric and then dampening it. I have discovered to my horror that some are labeled incorrectly. Be sure to leave 2 to 4 inches of mesh on all sides of the artwork for blocking and finishing.

PREPARING FABRIC FOR STITCHERY

To prevent fabric from unraveling as you work, bind all raw edges before you begin. The traditional approach for embroidery is to make neatly rolled and stitched hems. Plan your project so that the selvage, which will not need binding, is on the left side of your stitching.

Do not attempt to hem stiff fabrics such as needlepoint or rug canvas, as you will be constantly annoyed by the remaining raw edge, which will catch your yarn as you work. Instead, consider stitching bias seam tape or strips of scrap material over the raw edges of the mesh.

Taping, for me, is the best solution to edge binding because it is fast and efficient. For delicate materials, fold 1½″-wide masking tape over the raw edges. For a firm grip on heavyweight fabrics and canvas mesh, use masking tape or electrical tape at least 2″ wide. Both tapes are available in hardware stores.

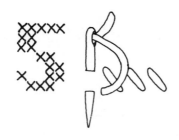

Stitches

AN INTRODUCTION FOR BEGINNERS

Many needlework stitches are so basic that even if you are holding a needle and thread for the first time, you will find them easy to learn. Knowing their traditional structure should help you refine your stitching technique and make your needlework neat, even, and strong. The following descriptions are given to suggest to you new directions in stitchery. You will find great satisfaction when you go beyond the very simple into the inventive.

There may be some stitches that seem frustratingly complicated at first. You may wonder if you will ever master them. Look carefully at the instructions and drawings. Practice on scrap fabric. If all else fails, ask an experienced friend for help or request assistance at a local needlework shop. You'll be pleased at how easy it is to do even the most complicated stitchery once you know how.

All stitch directions and illustrations for embroidery are given for right-handed people. Lefties may work in the opposite direction, provided they make sure the overall structure of their completed stitching is the same as shown. Some left-handed people may prefer holding a mirror up to the artwork as an aid when learning new stitches.

29

Needle and Thread Techniques

Although the basic mechanics of stitchery will become second nature to you as you gain experience, here is some basic information to help ensure your enjoyment and success.

Threading the Needle

To begin, cut your thread or yarn to a length just shorter than your arm, usually about 20 inches. This is a length established by experienced needle-workers as the most efficient. Longer thread will tangle more easily, while shorter thread will be used up too quickly.

Choose a needle with an eye roomy enough to hold your thread or yarn but not excessively large. The choice is always relative to the size of your materials because oversized needles are cumbersome to use and make unnecessarily large holes that may scar your fabric.

When using thread or floss, moisten the tip slightly, mold it into a point, and stab it through the eye of the needle. This is usually a straightforward procedure.

Wool, because of its uneven texture, can be harder to thread. First run your fingers along the length of the yarn to determine which direction is smooth and which is rough. If you thread the needle with the smooth side pointing into the eye, it should slide in easily and fray less as you stitch. In addition, for easy threading, fold back the end of the yarn about an inch, hold it in place, and flatten it between your thumb and forefinger. Then wiggle the folded yarn back and forth until a small amount passes through the needle's eye. Pull the yarn through the rest of the way with your fingers. If some of the strands stay behind, you will have to remove the yarn and begin the procedure again.

Beginning and Ending

Fasten the first thread of an embroidery project by making a small knot or taking a small backstitch on the underside of the fabric. Whichever method you choose, be sure there is nothing visible on the surface of the stitchery.

By far the best method, however—also appropriate for needlepoint—is to leave a tail of thread or yarn 1½ to 2 inches long on the back of the fabric and anchor it in position as you work by covering it with stitchery. When using this technique, be sure that the thread to be fastened does not become tangled up with your new stitchery and that it does not accidentally get drawn to the surface of the needlework. Fasten all successive new threads by weaving them carefully into the back of the existing stitchery.

For embroidery, end off when your thread becomes too short, or when you want to change colors, by making a few backstitches on the underside of the fabric into the completed stitches. For needlepoint, end off your yarn by weaving the needle and yarn in and out of the existing stitchery, also on the back of the needlework.

AN INTRODUCTION FOR THE EXPERIENCED

If you are experienced in one form of needlework, you will find it easy to make the transition into another type. The hardest part is becoming accustomed to bulky yarn and needles if you are used to using delicate materials, or vice versa. The stitches themselves, you will be delighted to discover, are basically the same. The resulting needlework will, of course, be very different, according to the materials and stitches you use.

EMBROIDERY

Cross-stitch

Structure

Cross-stitch is the classic stitch of sampler making. One of the simplest of all embroidery stitches, it has been used for centuries by people all over the world. Although there are many approaches to making cross-stitches, there are several timeless structural guidelines that you should follow to keep your needlework consistent and even.

Work all cross-stitches in one project over the same number of threads or mesh. If you have experience with cross-stitch, you may be able to break this rule with success to create special effects, but for the newcomer breaking this rule can only cause trouble.

No matter what the backing material—hardanger, Aida, burlap, gingham, or any other—be sure that the completed stitches all have the same surface structure. The direction in which you work, from right to left, left to right, top to bottom, or the reverse, isn't important. The top stroke of the cross-stitch must, however, always run from the bottom left diagonally to the upper right of a thread intersection if your work is to look regular and even.

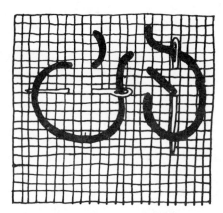

CROSS-STITCH.

Cross-stitches completed one at a time will look the most even.

Procedure

Here are two primary approaches to making cross-stitches.

METHOD 1 For the most even effect, complete each cross-stitch in its entirety before going on to the next. The first stroke runs from lower right to upper left. The second, or top stitch, crosses it from lower left to upper right.

METHOD 2 For faster stitching, work tent stitches (half cross-stitches) in one line or area as shown. Complete the stitches with a return trip of stitching.

A Special Note to Beginners and the Chronically Absentminded: If you are new at cross-stitching or, like me, often lose track of what you are doing no matter how much experience you have, fill out your cross-stitch design with tent stitches first, as described above. When you are sure that the color and stitch placement is correct, complete the cross-stitches. This technique saves a lot of time and aggravation if you have to remove and alter any of your stitches.

Surface Cross-stitch

If you wish to make cross-stitches on fabric too fine or uneven for counting threads, such as delicate muslin or silk, first baste a lightweight penelope or waste scrim canvas in position on the fabric. Work your cross-stitches through both layers. Pull the stitches tightly as you work so they will sit flat when the surface canvas is removed. When your stitchery is complete, remove the mesh by carefully cutting away the canvas close up to the embroidery. This will shorten the lengths of thread to be pulled through the embroidery, disturbing the stitchery as little as possible. See information under Cross-stitch Baby Sampler on Superfine Linen, on page 77.

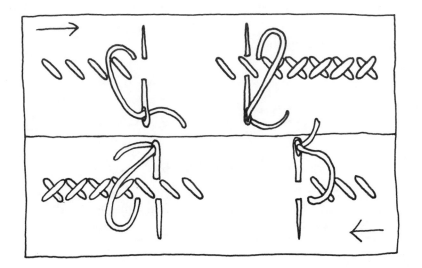

QUICK CROSS-STITCH.

To cover large areas or stitch long lines,
use the quick cross-stitch. Make the first
half of each stitch by working in one direction.
Complete the cross-stitches in a return trip.

Honest Mistakes

No one makes mistakes on purpose, and in cross-stitch it's easy to lose count of what you're doing. Although most errors are easily corrected, every once in a while you'll discover a mistake that is tightly surrounded by stitching. Such a mistake may not be worth removing. The procedure is time-consuming and dangerous, so examine your error carefully to see whether it affects the overall stitch count and composition. If not, leave it alone and continue with your needlework. What might seem to you like a glaring error will probably go unnoticed by other people. Honest, small imperfections contribute to the charm and humanity of a needlework project. To avoid major mistakes, make cross-stitches using Method 2, as previously described.

Running Stitch

Embroider the running stitch by weaving the needle and thread in and out of the fabric. Keep stitch lengths and the spaces between stitches as even as possible. In counted-thread embroidery, use the threads of the fabric as a guide to stitch length. Use the running stitch as a foundation for stitches such as the double running stitch, whipped running stitch, and pekinese stitch, shown in the following diagrams.

Double Running Stitch

Structure and Use

Double running stitch is perfect for outline work. Use it within a predominantly cross-stitch design to add important highlights that will prevent the cross-stitch from becoming overpowering and monotonous. Or use it by itself to create delicate, eye-catching images, such as those in the Sampler Baby Bib on page 144.

This stitch takes two trips across the needlework to complete. When you use it as part of a straight-line design, consider changing thread colors for the return trip. The double running stitch, when done correctly, is the same on the back of the fabric as on the front. Neat and attractive, it is ideal for decorating items that will be used without a backing, such as table linens or clothing.

First, make even running stitches around the outline of the design. Keep the length of the stitches and the spaces in between as even as possible by counting threads (or squares of gingham). To complete the stitch, turn your work and stitch back along the same line, filling in the spaces left by the first pass. For a good straight line, remember to insert the needle in the hole just above the stitch made on the first journey and bring it out again below that stitch as you work.

Backstitch

Structure and Use

You can also use the ordinary backstitch for simple or compact outline stitching when neatness on the fabric back is not important. Completed in one procedure, it is faster than the double running stitch and is especially useful for stitching simple letters such as those shown in the backstitch alphabet on page 19, and the Sampler Baby Bib on page 144.

Work from right to left. Begin by bringing the needle up a short distance to the left of the start of the line you wish to cover. Insert it to the right, at the beginning of the line. Bring it up again an equal distance forward along the line to the left. Continue working in this way, following the sequence of numbering in the Stitch Guide, until you have covered the desired area.

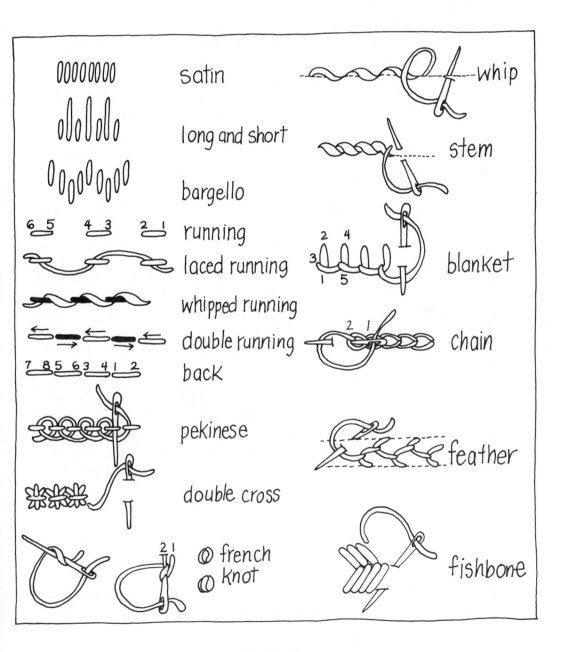

Stitch Guide.

Satin Stitch

Structure and Use

One of the most versatile and popular of all stitches, the satin stitch appears frequently in historic samplers, changing its name according to its use. Most commonly referred to by this name as an embroidery stitch, when used in needlepoint to create shaded geometric patterns it is called the Florentine or bargello stitch. Also known as gobelin, this is nothing more than a simple straight stitch. The long and short stitch, shown in the Stitch Guide, is a satin stitch variation.

Whether used on needlepoint canvas or embroidery fabric, it is good for filling in areas with solid texture. Although the procedure is simple, there are several pitfalls to consider, as described in the following section.

Procedure

For non-counted-thread fabric embroidery such as the Wise Old Owl Sampler on page 97, carry the thread across the area to be covered and bring it out again next to the starting point of the first stitch. Place each new stitch higher or lower than the previous one as needed, but be sure to keep the stitches right next to each other.

It is tempting to cover an area quickly with satin stitches that are too long or bulky. But long, heavy stitches on a delicate backing look awkward and do not wear well. Use a hoop or frame to keep your fabric taut and your stitches neat.

For counted-thread embroidery or needlepoint, use the threads of the fabric or mesh to make consistent parallel stitches. Use a frame to keep the mesh rigid and square.

For Florentine embroidery, or bargello, draw the needle over 4 threads of canvas and bring it up in position for the next stitch. Create different patterns and effects of shading by altering the number of threads you cover. Although bargello is most commonly done today on needlepoint canvas, it was often used in historic samplers on linen in combination with other embroidery stitches. The Family Sampler on page 66 includes areas of bargello stitchery.

Long and Short Stitch

Shown in the Stitch Guide, the long and short stitch is, as its name implies, a series of alternating long and short satin stitches.

French Knot

Fun and fast to do, the french knot has its own special look, which blends beautifully with all types of needlework. Use french knots one at a time to create tiny flowers or cluster them in groups to add whimsical texture.

To make a french knot, bring your needle and thread to the front of your fabric where you want to position the knot. Hold the needle near the surface of the fabric and wrap the thread around it with your free hand. Hold the thread firmly and return the needle to the back of the fabric by inserting it right next to the spot where it emerged. Pull the needle through to the back, leaving the knot on the front of the fabric.

If your needle is much thicker than your thread or yarn, the knot will slip through the hole it makes. To correct this problem, choose a smaller needle.

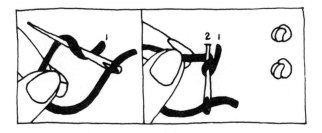

French Knot

NEEDLEPOINT

Although the following stitches are most often associated with needlepoint, the continental, or tent, stitch is also appropriate for counted-thread embroidery. The Train Sampler on page 73 is done with continental stitches on hardanger cloth.

Embroidery stitches such as satin stitch, previously described, work well on needlepoint mesh. Counted-thread satin stitch is called Florentine or bargello; see under "Satin Stitch" for information.

The instructions and diagrams for needlepoint that follow are intended for right-handed people. If you are left-handed, use the drawings by turning the book upside down or by placing the book in front of a mirror, as suggested earlier. A right-handed person will start most stitches at the base of the stitch. A left-handed person will start at the top. In doing this, a left-handed stitcher can duplicate the important stitch structure in a way that feels more natural.

Continental Stitch

Structure

The continental stitch is worked from right to left in straight lines, covering both sides of the canvas with a diagonal pattern. Use it on mono or interlock needlepoint canvas or even-weave counted-thread fabrics.

Procedure

To make the continental stitch, work the first row from right to left, stitching diagonally over the mesh, as shown. When you reach the end of the row, turn the canvas upside down and work back in the other direction. Pull the yarn gently against the mesh as you work. Too much tension will quickly distort the canvas and weaken the yarn.

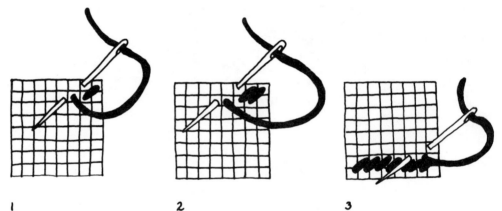

1   2   3

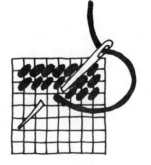

4   5

Continental Stitch.

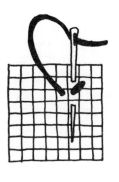

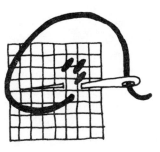

1   2   3

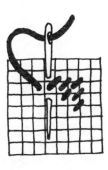
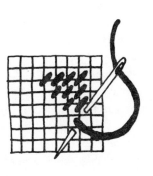

Basketweave Stitch.

4   5

Basketweave Stitch

Structure

The basketweave stitch looks exactly like the continental stitch on the surface, but the structure is quite different. The basketweave is more challenging to learn than the continental stitch, but it has two important advantages. Worked in ascending and descending diagonal rows, it covers the back of the needlepoint canvas with an interwoven structure that is strong and distributes the tension of the stitching more evenly than the continental stitch does. Large areas of canvas worked in basketweave are significantly less distorted than canvas worked in continental. For stitching in tight places or in straight lines, use the continental stitch, but for backgrounds and other large areas, use the basketweave.

Procedure

Begin the basketweave in the upper right-hand corner of the design or canvas. Be careful to alternate your ascending and descending rows so your stitches always mesh smoothly. Descending stitches will leave a vertical line on the back of the canvas. Ascending stitches make a horizontal line.

Starting in the upper right-hand corner, bring the needle from the back of the canvas to the front as if you were making the continental stitch. Bring the needle diagonally over the mesh intersection and down again through the upper-right hole, as shown. Row 1 is now complete.

Row 2 is a descending row. Make the first stitch immediately to the left of stitch 1. The second stitch of Row 2 falls directly below stitch 1. Row 2 is now complete.

Row 3 ascends. Make the first stitch in Row 3 directly below the last stitch in Row 2, as shown. Make the second stitch in Row 3 in the open space between the two stitches in Row 2. Make the third stitch immediately to the left of the first stitch in Row 2. Row 3 is complete.

Although these directions may seem confusing, what you are doing is setting up an arrangement of interwoven stitches as you begin and end rows of stitching. At the same time, the stitches are beginning to define the top and right side of a square. As the rows get longer, the stitch placement becomes more obvious. Basketweave can be frustrating until you master it, so if your first attempt creates a tangle of yarn instead of a neat little pattern of stitching, carefully cut the yarn away from the mesh and begin again. Be assured that basketweave has its own logical structure, which will become clear to you once you get beyond the initial confusion. Each diagonal row, whether ascending or descending, is composed of stitches in a staggered, broken line. This line will be filled in neatly when the next row returns in the opposite direction.

When starting a new strand of yarn, be sure to continue this alternating pattern, because going in the wrong direction will create an unpleasant ridge in your stitching. If you have trouble remembering whether to ascend or descend, consider changing strands in the middle of a row where the stitch direction is clearly indicated. You can also determine the appropriate stitch direction by studying the weave of the yarn on the back of the canvas.

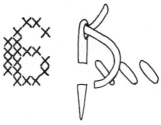

Finishing
Needlework

PRESSING EMBROIDERY

If you have been careful about your work habits, your embroidered sampler will probably need only pressing when the stitching is complete. To press embroidery, place a clean towel on your ironing surface. Lay the embroidery face down on the towel. Dampen the back of the sampler with clean water, using a clean sponge or hand pump sprayer. To avoid spotting, cover the whole fabric with moisture, not just the embroidered area. Now cover the sampler with a clean towel and press with a warm iron. You will be able to correct slight fabric puckering with pressing. To block embroidery that is badly puckered, see the following section on "Blocking Embroidery."

WASHING EMBROIDERY

Wash soiled embroidery with caution in lukewarm water, with mild soap. Knead the fabric gently and rinse in cool water. If water becomes colored, keep rinsing in fresh water until it stays clear. Never scrub, wring, or twist embroidery. Do final rinse in cold water. Carefully press out excess water with your hands and roll the embroidery in a clean, dry terrycloth towel. When the towel becomes saturated, move the sampler to a dry one. Lay the sampler out flat to dry face down on a clean surface away from direct sunlight. Iron carefully, as described above, while embroidery is slightly damp.

CLEANING EMBROIDERY

Consider having soiled embroidery cleaned by a reputable dry cleaner, but be sure to discuss the materials with the proprietor before leaving your embroidery. He or she may advise first testing sample materials for color fastness.

BLOCKING EMBROIDERY

Finished embroidery seldom needs the same thorough blocking as needlepoint, but if your embroidery is badly puckered, you can block it back into shape. To do this, lay it out, face down, on a wooden board covered with clean brown paper, as for needlepoint (see next section). Moisten the back of the fabric slightly with water from a clean sponge or hand pump sprayer. With a staple gun, thumbtacks, pushpins, or T pins, attach the embroidery to the covered board. Ease out bulges with the side of your hand as you work. Use only rustproof staples, thumbtacks, pushpins, or T pins and attach them at least an inch away from the stitchery as a precaution. If the fabric is fragile, place masking tape along the edges and staple or tack into this. Embroidery will not need—and cannot withstand—the same intense stretching as needlepoint, so be firm but gentle as you work. Allow your stretched embroidery to dry overnight or longer if needed.

BLOCKING NEEDLEPOINT

Finished needlepoint, especially when worked in your lap without a frame, is often misshapen when the stitching is complete. Be sure to block it back into shape or have it done at a local needlework shop before it is mounted or stitched into a pillow or rug.

If you are a prolific needlepointer it will be worthwhile for you to invest in supplies and spend time blocking your own work. If you stitch only the Quick Point Sampler Rug on page 103, consider having your needlepoint finished for you in a reliable neighborhood needlework shop.

Materials for Blocking Needlepoint

Since many of the supplies you will need for blocking needlepoint are expensive, you might borrow them from a friend before you decide to invest. Here's what you will need:

Large clean wooden board or piece of pressboard with straight edges
Sheet of clean brown paper, taped to the board
Staple gun, tacks, pushpins, or T pins, rustproof
Metal T square or right-angle

Blocking Technique

Dampen the back of your finished needlepoint with a clean wet sponge, hand pump sprayer, or other method. Saturate the needlework only enough to soften the sizing, not wash it away. Shake off any excess moisture.

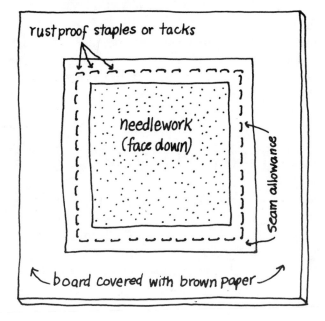

Blocking needlework

rustproof staples or tacks

needlework
(face down)

Seam allowance

board covered with brown paper

Place dampened, limp needlepoint face down in the center of the board, which has been covered with clean paper. Put several staples or pins into the top edge of the needlepoint mesh, leaving a row or two of mesh between the edge of the stitchery and the staples.

Pull the needlepoint firmly and put several more staples along the bottom edge, reestablishing your grip after each staple, if needed. Use the T square or right-angle as a guide for pulling the edges straight and squaring the corners.

While you should have no trouble pulling and stapling two sides and part of a third into straight, parallel lines, you will have to pull firmly to control the last side and a half. If the mesh slips as you staple, remove the staples carefully, using the tool provided on the staple gun or a blunt kitchen knife, and stretch again.

Needlepoint that is excessively misshapen may need several blockings. Each blocking will be easier, taking only about fifteen minutes of work.

Drying time may take anywhere from overnight to several days, depending on your environment. Be sure that your needlepoint is completely dry before removing it from the blocking board, because if it is still slightly damp it will slip back into a crooked shape.

NEEDLEPOINT RUGS AND WALL HANGINGS

You will probably want to have your needlepoint rug blocked and finished at your local needlework shop. If you decide to hang your rug rather than use it on the floor, sew plastic rings, bought at a variety store, at even intervals along the top of the rug binding and hang these on nails on the wall.

CONSTRUCTING NEEDLEPOINT PILLOWS

Once your needlepoint is blocked, you can stitch it into a knife-edge pillow as if it were any other flat fabric. Choose a heavyweight fabric for the pillow back, such as velvet, velveteen, corduroy, denim, or suede cloth. When trimming away excess fabric, trim the unworked canvas only. Do *not* cut into the stitchery. For a durable construction, be sure to include several rows of needlepoint stitching in your pillow seam allowance. For more on pillow construction, see following page.

WASHING AND REVITALIZING NEEDLEPOINT PILLOWS

Eventually your needlepoint will need cleaning. Put Woolite in a sink and run the cold water until the detergent is well dissolved and foamy. Use a clean sponge to scoop up some foam and gently draw it across the surface of the needlepoint. Wash out the sponge in cold water, wring out the excess moisture, and draw it across the needlepoint to remove the soap.

If you live in a high-activity household, as I do, you may find after several years that while your needlepoint pillows are dirty but in otherwise good shape, the pillow backs, especially the corners, are worn out. Find the hand-sewn area of the pillow seam and carefully remove the stitching with sharp embroidery scissors. Remove the stuffing and reverse the pillow. Remove the machine stitches carefully and discard the worn fabric. Staple the needlepoint *face up* to a clean blocking surface, as described under "Blocking Needlepoint," and wash it as described above. Remake the pillow with new fabric, as described in the next section. You can also have this work done at a local needlework shop.

CONSTRUCTING SAMPLER PILLOWS

Sampler pillows make great gifts for friends and relatives of all ages. Whether adorning a grandparent's couch or decorating a niece's or nephew's bed, or even placed on a chair in your own home, pillows are easy and satisfying to make.

The following instructions are for a two-sided knife-edge pillow, a classic pillow that is flattering to all forms of needlework. Although pillow construction can be done by hand, machine stitching, which is stronger, is best.

When your sampler is complete, press or block it, as needed, according to the preceding instructions in this chapter.

Preparation

Choose a strong fabric for the pillow backing in a color and texture that blend with your sampler. It should be the same size as the sampler, including seam allowance.

For lightweight pillows such as the Sampler Birthday Pillow, in gingham, on page 117, add a layer of muslin or white cotton under the back and front of the pillow for durability. To do this, cut 2 pieces of muslin to the same size as the finished needlework and attach 1 piece to the back of the stitchery and the other to the underside of the pillow backing fabric with crisscrossing basting lines. Be sure to smooth the layers together. If necessary, pin the layers together securely before basting to prevent them from buckling. Remove visible basting lines when the pillow is complete.

Procedure

When you are ready to begin pillow construction, decide where the outline of the pillow is to be and define it with basting lines. Use the threads of the fabric as a guide for basting straight lines and be sure to delineate the corners clearly. For needlepoint, stitch basting lines or use the lines of the stitches themselves as a guide since several rows of needlepoint stitching should be included in the pillow seam allowance, for strength.

Trim away excess fabric (except canvas) around the outside edge of the sampler pillow top, leaving at least an inch seam allowance on all sides. For needlepoint, trim unworked canvas mesh only. Do *not* cut into actual stitching, and be sure to leave at least 2 threads of canvas on all sides. Trim the backing fabric to the same size as the pillow front, including seam allowance.

1. Lay the pillow front and pillow back face to face, smooth out any bulges with the side of your hand, and pin together.
2. Stitch around the outside edges, using the basting line as a guide. For strength, backstitch at the beginning and end of the line of stitching. Include all four corners in your stitching, but leave an appropriately sized opening along the bottom edge for turning the pillow right side out. Bulky needlepoint will need at least a 3-inch opening, while lightweight gingham or hardanger will need less.
3. When the stitching is complete, trim the corners on the diagonal. Cut the backing mesh but do not cut into the stitching itself. Reverse the pillow.
4. Stuff the pillow with loose Dacron polyester fiberfill, available in fabric stores. Use a crochet hook or other blunt instrument to push the filling into the corners. Continue to add stuffing until you reach a satisfying density. Fold in the seam allowance of the remaining opening so that it matches the seam already sewn. Pin it in position and stitch closed by hand. Use tiny overhand stitches or blind stitches that are hidden in the seam.

Knife-edge pillow construction

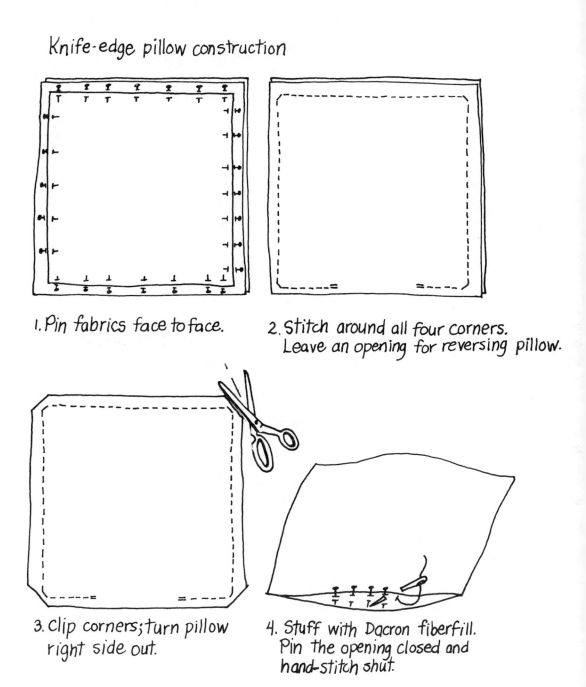

1. Pin fabrics face to face.

2. Stitch around all four corners. Leave an opening for reversing pillow.

3. Clip corners; turn pillow right side out.

4. Stuff with Dacron fiberfill. Pin the opening closed and hand-stitch shut.

CONSTRUCTING SAMPLER QUILTS

Quilting is the technique of joining three layers of material together to make a stronger, warmer fabric. Although the basic stitch is a simple running stitch, which you can do by hand or machine, learning to keep the layers of fabric smooth and flat as you work takes preparation and practice. Beginners will find quilting easier on smaller projects, such as pillows, since there is less bulk to control. Once you have mastered the technique on a small scale, you will be better prepared to complete a larger, more cumbersome quilt. The following instructions are appropriate for projects of any size, from pillows to bedspreads.

Fabrics for Quilting

Three layers of fabric make up the sandwich you will be quilting. To complete a sampler quilt, here's what you will need:

Quilt Top

Use a sampler, complete with any additional trimming desired.

Filling or Interlining

Buy Dacron polyester quilt batting, available in precut standard bedspread sizes, at a local fabric shop. For a pillow or small quilt, choose batting packaged for a baby quilt and cut down to size. You may also use flannel or a lightweight blanket. Bulkier fillings are difficult to stitch neatly.

Backing

Choose a lightweight cotton backing in a solid or print that coordinates with your quilt top. For quilted sampler pillows, where the backing will be hidden in the pillow construction, use muslin or other lightweight inexpensive cotton fabric.

Other Supplies

For quilting you will also need straight pins, scissors, basting thread, waxed quilting thread (available in fabric shops), a quilting needle of "in-between" size (7–9), a thimble, and masking tape. For the Gingham Sampler Quilt on page 129 you will need a pencil, tracing paper, and shirt cardboard.

The quilting frame or hoop is also an important aid for hand quilting. People who do a great deal of quilting use large, free-standing frames, but I prefer the less expensive quilting hoop, which is portable and easy to store away when not in use. It is available in local fabric and needlework stores. For very small hand-quilting projects, use an embroidery hoop if the filling isn't too bulky.

For fast, strong contemporary quilting, use a sewing machine. Assemble the layers as described in the following sections, but use machine straight stitches instead of handwork. Use both hand stitching and machine quilting to complete the Gingham Sampler Quilt.

Assembling the Layers

Laying out the layers to be quilted so they are smooth and even is as important as the stitching itself. Prepare all materials (except the quilt batting) by pressing out bulges and wrinkles.

On a clear, smooth, hard surface, spread out the backing fabric, face down. If your project is large—a full-sized quilt, for example—work on the floor. Lay the quilt batting (the interlining) on top of this and ease out any bulges with the side of your hand. Next place the decorative sampler top over the first two layers, face up. Smooth out any bulges, working from the center of the needlework out toward the edges. Leave a 2-inch margin of backing fabric and interlining sticking out from all sides of the top layer. If you find that the fabrics are shifting out of control as you work, use masking tape to anchor the edges of each layer.

To prevent the layers from shifting and buckling later as you quilt, pin and baste them together before beginning to stitch. Pinning alone may be adequate for smaller projects, but larger quilt sandwiches and machine-quilted projects will almost certainly need to be basted with long running stitches. Be sure your pins or basting stitches catch all three layers of the quilt sandwich. Again, to avoid bulges, always start from the center and work toward the outside edges.

When you are confident that the layers are anchored firmly, you may begin to stitch, working, as before, from the center outward. Remove pins and basting slowly, as they get in the way of your permanent stitching.

 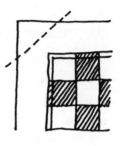

1. Lay out backing fabric,
   face down.
2. Center and smooth
   out interlining.
3. Center completed
   quilt top, face up.

4. Join layers with machine
   or hand quilting.
5. Trim corners on
   the diagonal.

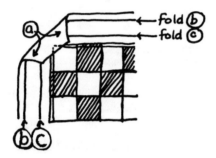 

6. Fold corners of backing
   fabric over quilt top (a).
7. Fold over narrow hem (b).
8. Fold over wide hem (c).

9. Pin securely.
10. Machine zigzag or straight
    stitch in position.

EASY QUILT CONSTRUCTION WITH MITERED CORNERS.

Quilting by Hand

The quilting stitch is a tiny running stitch spaced evenly on both the top of
the needlework and the underside. Learning to control the size and placement of the stitches on a sophisticated quilt project while keeping your
layers smooth can be challenging, so if you are a beginner try to make 5 or
6 stitches per inch on the surface of your needlework. As you gain experience, refine your stitching.

Secure the quilt layers face up in a frame or hoop, as previously mentioned. Thread the needle with a single strand of quilting thread, approximately the length of your arm. Knot the end.

Bring the needle and thread straight up from the underside through the layers and gently tug the knot past the backing fabric into the interlining. It may take practice until you learn how much pressure is needed. When the knot is in place, make a backstitch to keep it secure. Then begin to quilt, using one of the following methods.

In the first method, make a running stitch in two separate strokes. With one hand, send the needle through the layers at right angles to the surface. Receive it with the other hand, pull it through, and return it at the same 90-degree angle. You will have the best control of your stitches when you use this method, although it can be painfully slow.

Begin a line of quilting by securing the first stitch with a backstitch.

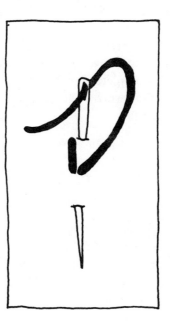

Quilting the layers

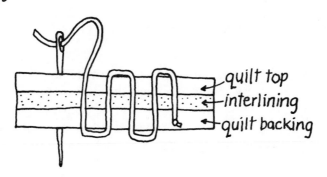

quilt top
interlining
quilt backing

To work faster, bring the needle up from the underside and fasten the knot as described. Then catch several stitches on the needle before pulling it through the fabric. Do all of your work on the quilt surface. Be sure you have caught all the layers of the quilt sandwich on the needle before pulling it through, as missing fabric is one of the pitfalls of this technique.

Machine Quilting

To quilt by machine, use standard sewing thread in the sewing machine needle and bobbin. Set the machine for 12 to 14 straight stitches per inch. Wherever possible, work from the center of the design outward to help avoid puckering. Machine-stitch along the appropriate lines, removing any basting as it interferes. Begin and end each line with a backstitch to fasten the thread. Wherever a line ends, stop stitching, secure the thread with a backstitch, and move the needle to the beginning of a new line. When stitching is complete, remove all remaining basting. Pull gently on bobbin threads to draw surface threads left by the needle to the back of the fabric, and trim carefully.

Finishing Quilt Edges

When all quilting is complete, trim the corners, and bind and stitch the edges of the quilt by folding the sides and mitering the edges, as shown in the illustration "Easy quilt construction with mitered corners." For durability, machine zigzag or straight stitching works best, even if the interior quilting has been done by hand.

How to Use Quilting

When used with discretion, quilting can contribute the finishing touch to many simple projects. By quilting through several layers of fabric, you will strengthen the fabric and create an illusion of shadow and volume. The hand-quilted hearts, traced in position with chalk and a cardboard template on the Gingham Sampler Quilt (page 129), enhance the importance of the delicate cross-stitch gingham squares. The Gingham Sampler Quilt is a large, cumbersome project for a beginner. If you are a newcomer to stitchery, consider first making a scaled-down version of this quilt, such as a baby quilt or pillow top.

For fast, satisfying results easy enough for a beginner, place machine straight stitching along the edge of a patchwork border. This technique, also used in the Gingham Sampler Quilt, can add a rich dimension to an otherwise flat area.

MOUNTING AND FRAMING SAMPLERS

Even though you love doing needlework, you may not be interested in mounting and framing your own sampler. Have the work done at a reliable frame or needlework shop. Talk to the proprietors about their techniques and ask to see examples of mounted needlework. Leave your own stitchery for mounting and framing only if you feel satisfied that they are experienced in needlework mounting procedures.

If you are an adventurous craftsperson, you may want to mount and frame your sampler at home. Instructions follow in this chapter.

Display Aesthetics

The greatest injustice you can perpetrate on your beautiful needlework is to display it poorly. Whether you mount and frame your work inexpensively at home or have it done by a professional, the pitfalls are the same. The following suggestions apply, no matter who does the actual work.

Although many old samplers are crowded into frames, the ones with an extra margin of space left on all sides look the most graceful. An empty area left around the outside edges will enhance the look of your sampler, too. Consider adding a border of velvet or satin ribbon, in the style of the historic samplers, or add patchwork fabric borders, as shown on page 160.

Many samplers in this collection—such as the Hardanger Baby Sampler on page 62—are designed with needlework border motifs. But even these look best when framed with several inches of fabric left visible on all sides. The Quick Point Sampler Rug (page 103) and the Needlepoint House Sampler Pillow (page 113) have their own needlework border effects. For more ideas on attractive display techniques, look through the color section. Add all stitched border trim before mounting. Also consider using a cardboard mat, as described on page 58.

Pitfalls to Avoid

If you frame your sampler under glass, avoid the glareproof kind. It will flatten the color and detract from the richness of the stitching.

Do not mount or frame your sampler with anything that will leave permanent scars. Do not cut your sampler too close to the stitchery, and do not use glue. Use only acid-free board or paper, available in art supply stores, to avoid eventual stains in the sampler fabric. Use only rustproof tacks, nails, or staples and apply them well away from the stitching.

Materials for Sampler Mounting

Completed sampler (with fabric borders, if any)
⅜" chipboard, foam-core board, Masonite, or plywood
Mat knife (for cutting chipboard or foam-core)

> or

Saw (for cutting heavier board—or have board cut at a lumberyard)
Metal straightedge
Heavy-duty staple gun with ¼" rustproof staples

> or

¼" rustproof tacks and hammer
Pushpins (optional)
Acid-free paper or board (optional)

Be sure to read through the following sections before you begin to work.

Preparing Needlework for Mounting

Determine the area you wish to have visible on your finished sampler, as described under "Display Aesthetics," earlier. Put in long basting lines along each side of the completed sampler, using the woven threads of the fabric as a guide. Count threads if needed. While this is a time-consuming job, it will enable you to mount your sampler squarely.

Mounting Board

Using a sharp mat knife and metal straightedge, cut ⅜″ chipboard or foam-core board to the same size as the area indicated with basting lines on your sampler. You may also use Masonite or plywood if you place thin chipboard or other acid-free paper between the board and needlework before final mounting.

If you plan to frame your finished sampler, mount it on chipboard. If you prefer to mount and hang your sampler without a frame, use foam-core board, Masonite, or plywood. Samplers stretched on chipboard left without support will warp.

Fastening the Sampler to the Board

A heavy-duty staple gun with short, rustproof staples is the most efficient tool for mounting samplers. Although expensive, it is a worthwhile investment if you plan to mount a lot of stitchery. You may also use rustproof tacks, which are much less costly but considerably more difficult to manipulate. Also consider the traditional method of sampler mounting, lacing. All techniques are described below.

Mounting Procedure—Using Staples or Tacks

Step 1

Place the sampler face down on a clean, hard surface. Center a board, cut to size as described above, in the area indicated by the basting lines. If using Masonite or plywood, sandwich acid-free paper between sampler and board.

Step 2

Fold one edge of the fabric over the board and attach to the board with rustproof staples or rustproof tacks, placed every ½ inch. To avoid buckling of the fabric, work from the center of one side outward. Whether you use staples or tacks, be sure they are shorter than the board is deep so that they do not come through the front of the board and the needlework.

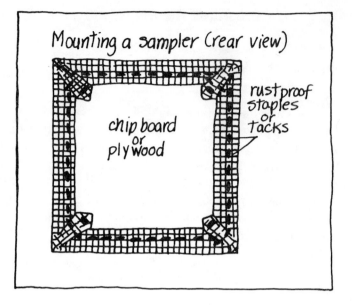

Mounting a sampler (rear view)

rustproof staples or tacks

chip board or plywood

Step 3

Fold the fabric on the opposite edge over the board. Again, working from the center outward, apply staples, pulling the fabric taut.

Step 4

Use the same procedure to attach the sides. Fold the corners neatly before you apply staples too close to them and fasten corners with staples.

Step 5

If your mounting is imperfect in any way, don't be afraid to remove the staples with care and reattach.

Mounting Procedure—Lacing

Lacing, the traditional method of sampler mounting, is the least expensive technique, although it is the most difficult to perfect.

Preparation

Be sure all edges of the sampler base fabric are bound or hemmed securely.

Place basting lines around the outer boundaries of the sampler, as previously described. Choose an appropriate board and cut it to size.

Step 1

Place the sampler face down on a hard surface and center the board on it, using basting lines to guide placement. Sandwich acid-free paper between sampler and board if necessary.

Step 2

Wrap the fabric around the board and fasten on the back temporarily with pushpins, available in art supply stores.

Step 3

Use a needle and carpet thread or crochet cotton to attach the facing edges with long stitches. Work from side to side and top to bottom. Be sure the face of the sampler is pulled evenly, without bulges.

Step 4

Fold the corners neatly and fasten temporarily with pins. Include the corners in the lacing. Remove all pins.

Step 5

If the sampler is buckled or off center in any way, remove lacing and re-attach.

lacing

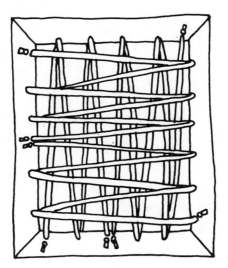

Mats for Picture Frames

You may want to use a cardboard mat, or inner frame, when you frame your sampler. Mats cut from acid-free board offer added protection to your sampler while providing a small breathing space between the surface of the stitchery and the glass. Since good mat cutting is a skill that takes practice, you may want to have one cut at an art store or frame shop.

To cut your own mat, buy good-quality mat board from an art supply store. Select a shade that will blend with your sampler. Colors that are too bright overwhelm stitchery.

In addition to mat board, you will also need a long metal ruler, a pencil, and a sharp mat knife or utility knife. Work on a hard, flat surface protected by cardboard or a pile of newspapers.

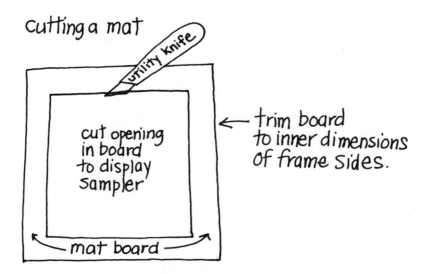

Procedure for Making a Mat

Step 1

Cut the board down to the inner dimensions of the frame sides. See the following section for frame information.

Step 2

On the wrong side of the board, measure and mark with a pencil the rectangular or square area you wish to cut out for sampler display. The mat opening should be slightly smaller than the sampler so that the sampler doesn't fall through it.

Step 3

Make tiny, deep cuts with the point of the mat knife in each corner of the mat, to define them.

Step 4

Holding the metal ruler firmly in place with one hand, use the mat knife to make a long, straight cut along one side of the rectangle, following the drawn line. You may have to make several strokes before you pierce the board completely, but make each pass in a continuous motion to keep the cut clean.

Step 5

When all sides are cut, remove the center rectangle and discard. Use the cardboard frame or mat inside a frame, as described in the next section.

FRAMING SAMPLERS

You may want to have your sampler mounted and framed by a local shop or you may want to do the work yourself for economy and satisfaction. Framing mounted needlework is not difficult, although, as with mounting, there are several options to consider.

If your mounted needlework is a standard size (such as 8″×10″ or 9″×12″), you will be able to buy an inexpensive frame in a local art supply or variety store. The framed samplers in this book are, however, displayed in custom-cut frames. Although they are more expensive, custom-made frames will age gracefully while they complement and protect your stitchery. Take your time when choosing a frame; most framers offer such a wide variety that selecting a molding can be overwhelming. Also, be sure to select a frame that is deep enough for needlework.

Frame shops will prefer to do the entire fitting and finishing of the sampler and the frame, but to save money you can also do the job at home.

Here is a list of what you will need:

Finished sampler, mounted
Frame
Glass, cut to size
1″ brads, tacks, or staple gun
Small hammer
Brown kraft paper
White glue
Newspapers
Rubbing alcohol
Pencil
Acid-free mat board (optional)
Chipboard or shirt cardboard (optional)
Metal ruler
Mat knife
2 screw eyes
Picture-hanging wire
Wire cutters

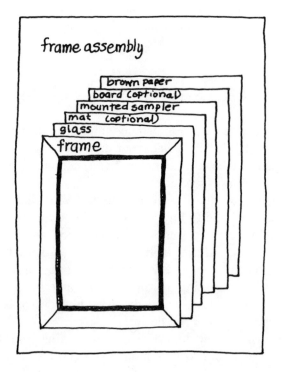

Procedure

Step 1

Lay out newspaper on a flat, hard surface. Clean both sides of glass. To do this, use strips of newspaper and rubbing alcohol. The ink of the newsprint and the alcohol combined together help the glass dry free of streaks. Handle the edges of the glass with scraps of newspaper to protect your fingers and prevent leaving fingerprints. Inspect both sides of the glass in sunlight or under a lamp. Place the cleaned glass on newspaper and allow it to dry thoroughly.

Step 2

Place the frame face down on a clean area of newspaper. Insert the glass in the frame. Check to see that no scraps or lint have fallen on the glass.

Step 3 (Optional)

(Omit mat, if preferred.) Insert the mat, face down, in the frame. Instructions for mat cutting are in previous section. Place the mounted sampler face down in the frame. Place acid-free board or paper cut to same size over back of sampler, if there is room.

Step 4

Fasten the sampler in the frame by placing several brads, tacks, or staples in the inner edges of the wood frame molding. Keep staples or tacks as parallel to sampler as possible.

Step 5

Spread a small amount of white glue on the back of the frame, but avoid the sampler. Smooth brown kraft paper, trimmed to slightly larger than the frame, over the back of the frame. When the glue is completely dry, use the metal ruler and mat knife to trim the edges of the paper even with the edges of the frame.

Step 6

Insert screw eyes on the back of the frame, one on each side, just above the center. Thread a length of wire through the eyes and twist excess wire around itself several times to secure.

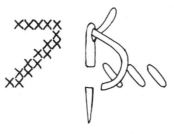

The Samplers

A NOTE ON MEASUREMENT VARIATIONS

Because so-called even-weave fabrics are often not as perfect as the name implies, and because stitchery styles vary from person to person, actual fabric measurements and material amounts may vary slightly from those given for each project. Be sure to leave ample seam allowances on all fabrics because even those designs you intend to follow exactly may vary by an inch or two when complete. Be ready to make adjustments as needed, knowing that this is part of the stitchery process and will make your own work distinctly personal.

HARDANGER BABY SAMPLER

Finished size: 14"×12½" (plus frame)

This graceful sampler was designed and stitched by Vicki Rosenberg in celebration of the birth of my son Jesse. It was a thrilling gift to receive, and it was especially exciting to watch Jesse become fascinated with the delicately stitched cats and birds.

Vicki, who has been stitching wonderful samplers for several years as gifts for lucky family members and friends, keeps a file of her favorite motifs, which she consults whenever she begins a new project.

Materials Needed

Off-white hardanger cloth, 24 threads to the inch, 15″×14″ or size appropriate to your project, plus seam allowance, edges basted or taped

⚹8 DMC pearl cotton, 1 ball in each of the following colors:

  light pink ⚹754
  medium pink ⚹352
  dark pink ⚹350
  light green ⚹955
  dark green ⚹3346
  light blue ⚹3325
  dark blue ⚹322
  light yellow ⚹744
  bright yellow ⚹725
  brown ⚹433
  red ⚹321
  lavender ⚹210

Embroidery needle
Scissors
Graph paper and pencil
Embroidery hoop
Hand sewing needle
Basting thread
Masking tape

HARDANGER BABY SAMPLER.

Color key for Hardanger Baby Sampler:

○	LIGHT BLUE		R	MEDIUM PINK
●	DARK BLUE		Y	LIGHT YELLOW
∕	LIGHT GREEN		▼	BRIGHT YELLOW
⊠	DARK GREEN		L	LAVENDER
▷	RED		b	BROWN
R	DARK PINK		P	LIGHT PINK

Unusual Characteristics

Both the horizontal and the vertical borders have doubled-up stitches in the center of the lines of stitching to even the stitch count. Watch the chart carefully as you work, and keep this in mind as you adjust border lengths for your own needs. You may be able to eliminate the extra stitches.

Preparation

Using the alphabet shown on page 17, chart on graph paper the name and date you wish to include in your sampler. Plan to lengthen and shorten borders to accommodate your needs, and chart these changes on graph paper, as shown on page 23.

Iron the fabric. Prepare fabric and artwork by marking center lines with basting, as described in centering section on page 22.

Procedure

Step 1

Using the accompanying sampler chart and your own charted information, begin to cross-stitch in the center of the sampler and work out toward the edges. For more on cross-stitch techniques, see page 31.

Use an embroidery hoop. Work with a single strand of ⁒8 pearl cotton over 4 threads of hardanger. Carefully remove sections of basting lines as they get in the way.

Step 2

When stitchery is complete, remove any remaining basting lines and iron sampler, as described on page 41.

Step 3

Finishing instructions are in Chapter Six, "Finishing Needlework." Press and mount sampler on board, leaving at least 2″ of hardanger fabric visible on all sides. Frame mounted sampler.

FAMILY SAMPLER

Finished size: 7¾"×13" (including frame)

Here's a fast, satisfying sampler to stitch. (For full view of this sampler, see the color section.) The long, narrow shape and the natural-color linen background combine to give this sampler the look of an antique. Find this fabric in your local needlework shop or order it from Boutique Margot. The address is given on page 4.

Chart your own personal and place names and date on graph paper before you trim the fabric and begin stitching. The decorative borders shown in the accompanying chart are tailored to fit the Webster Family, so count out the spaces you'll need from your own chart and extend or shorten lines as needed. For help with letter spacing, see page 21.

Materials Needed

Natural-color even-weave linen cloth, 14 threads to the inch, 8½"×14" or
   size appropriate to your project, edges basted or taped
⁙5 DMC pearl cotton, 1 ball in each of the following colors:
   scarlet ⁙350
   salmon ⁙352
   mint green ⁙913
   dark green ⁙909
   dark gray ⁙414
   light gray ⁙415
   bright yellow ⁙725
Embroidery needle
Scissors
Graph paper and pencil

FAMILY SAMPLER.

Determine border lengths according to the lengths of names in your sampler. Repeat or eliminate motifs as needed.

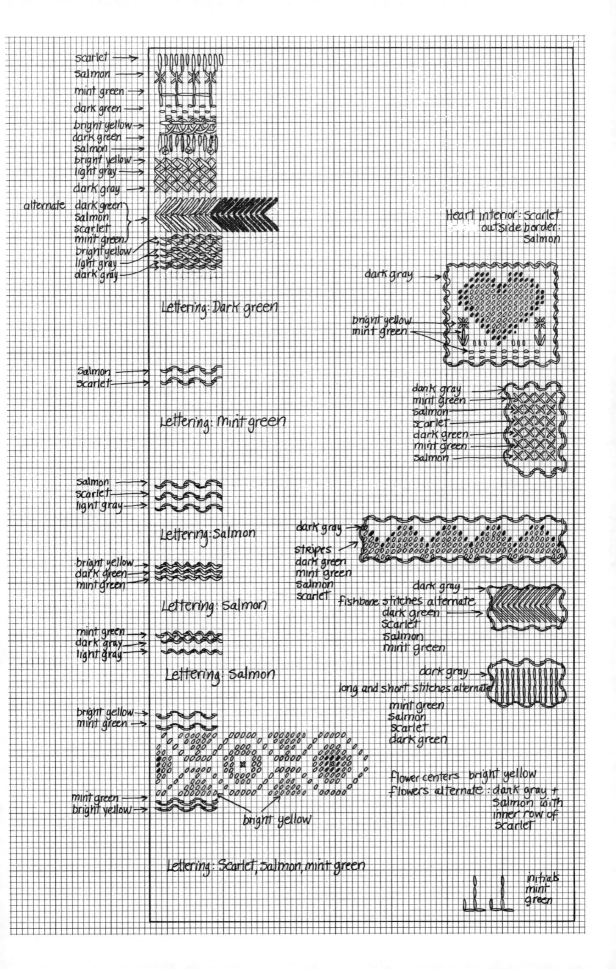

scarlet →
salmon →
mint green →
dark green →
bright yellow →
dark green →
salmon →
bright yellow →
light gray →
dark gray →

alternate { dark green }
salmon
scarlet
mint green }
bright yellow
light gray
dark gray

Lettering: Dark green

Heart interior: scarlet
outside border: Salmon

dark gray →

bright yellow
mint green

Salmon →
scarlet →

Lettering: mint green

dark gray
mint green
salmon
scarlet
dark green
mint green
salmon

salmon →
scarlet →
light gray →

Lettering: Salmon

dark gray →
stripes
dark green
mint green
salmon
scarlet

bright yellow
dark green →
mint green

Lettering: Salmon

dark gray →
Fishbone stitches alternate
dark green →
scarlet
salmon
mint green

mint green →
dark gray →
light gray →

Lettering: Salmon

dark gray →
long and short stitches alternate
mint green
Salmon
Scarlet
dark green

bright yellow →
mint green →

flower centers bright yellow
flowers alternate: dark gray +
salmon with
inner row of
scarlet

mint green →
bright yellow →

bright yellow

Lettering: Scarlet, salmon, mint green

initials
mint
green

Preparation

Using the alphabet shown on page 17, chart on graph paper the personal and place names and date you wish to include in your sampler. Count the threads and adjust the dimensions of the background fabric according to your needs.

Procedure

Step 1

Using the accompanying chart, begin at the top of the sampler and fill in rows of embroidery stitching. The stitches are, beginning at the top, the long and short stitch, double cross-stitch, straight stitch, running stitch, pekinese stitch, long and short stitch with french knot, cross-stitch, fishbone, and whipped running stitch.

Step 2

Use the cross-stitch over a single thread of fabric for all lettering. Use the laced running stitch between lines of words; use the continental stitch and cross-stitch for the repeating border embroidery farther down the sampler. Be sure to sign this project at the bottom with your own name or initials, using the backstitch alphabet on page 19. All other stitches are shown in Chapter Five, "Stitches."

Step 3

Finishing instructions are in Chapter Six, "Finishing Needlework."

Press and mount on board, leaving at least 6 rows of threads on each side. Frame mounted sampler.

NEW YORK CITY SAMPLER. (See page 70 for instructions)

Color key for New York City Sampler:

ⓑ	BEIGE	ⓝ	PINK
⊞	GRAY	Ⓨ	BRIGHT YELLOW
⊠	DARK GREEN	⊡	LIGHT BLUE
⊿	GRAY-GREEN	◉	DARK BLUE
⊏	LAVENDER	⊵	SCARLET

NEW YORK CITY SAMPLER

(See pages 68–69 for color key and chart)
Finished size: 12″×14″ (including patchwork borders)

Regina Larkin is a New York City–based dancer who likes to have a needlework project for the times she's traveling to work or waiting to rehearse
or perform. An avid knitter, she wanted to try a new technique. When I designed the New York City Sampler for her, she completed it in a few weeks
and was immediately ready for more of a challenge—see the Train Sampler,
which follows.

Materials Needed

Natural-color Aida cloth, 8 threads to the inch, 10″×12″, edges basted or
    taped
⋇5 DMC pearl cotton, 1 ball in each of the following colors:
    dark green ⋇701
    gray-green ⋇368
    bright yellow ⋇725
    scarlet ⋇350
    pink ⋇353
    light blue ⋇827
    gray ⋇318
    beige ⋇642
    lavender ⋇554
    dark blue ⋇334
For inner patchwork border:
    2 strips cotton fabric, each ¼″×10″, plus seam allowance
    2 strips cotton fabric, each ¼″×12″, plus seam allowance
For outer patchwork border:
    2 strips cotton fabric, each 2″×10″, plus seam allowance
    2 strips cotton fabric, each 2″×12″, plus seam allowance
Embroidery needle
Scissors
Graph paper and pencil
Embroidery hoop
Sewing machine

Unusual Characteristics

Although the simple shapes used in this sampler suggest New York City landmarks such as the Empire State and Citicorp buildings, you can easily make changes to reflect the city where you live. If you live in the country or suburbs, borrow a house design from the Hardanger Baby Sampler chart on page 64 or the Needlepoint House Sampler Pillow chart on page 112.

Some letters shown in the alphabet chart on page 19 are more compact than those used in the sampler stitchery. Choose letters according to your space needs and personal preference.

Preparation

Using the alphabet, as described above, chart your name and city name and date on graph paper. Plan any skyline adaptations, as suggested. Prepare fabric and artwork for stitching with basting lines, as shown on page 22.

Procedure

Step 1

Using the New York City Sampler chart and your own personal graphed information, begin cross-stitching at center of sampler and work outward. Use a single strand of pearl cotton over 4 strands of Aida cloth.

Step 2

When the stitching is complete, press or block embroidery as needed, as described on pages 41–44. Add basting lines around outside edge of sampler to define an 8″×10″ area.

Step 3: Adding Patchwork Borders

Cut and iron flowered cotton strips for patchwork borders according to the measurements given in the materials section. If you have changed the dimensions given for the sampler, adjust the border strips accordingly.

Step 4

Lay out completed sampler face up on flat surface with patchwork border strips in position. Remove a pair of inner and outer strips from the top edge of the sampler. Machine-stitch them together face to face. Press open and replace. Continue until all pairs have been joined and replaced in the layout.

Step 5

Attach patchwork borders by placing the top strip face to face with top edge of the sampler. Be sure the edge that is to be the inner border is flush with the line basted along the top of the sampler. Pin and machine-stitch ¼" outside the basting line. Join the bottom strip, using the same technique. Remove pins, open fabrics, and press flat. Add the side borders, using the same technique. To create patchwork borders with a different look, see the Sampler Tote on page 122.

Step 6

Remove all basting lines. Press the completed sampler and patchwork borders. Mount and frame according to the instructions beginning on page 53.

Adding patchwork borders to the New York City Sampler.

TRAIN SAMPLER

Finished size: 10″×8¾″ (plus frame)

By the time Regina Larkin had completed her first sampler (see the New York City Sampler, which precedes), she was excited about starting another. She gave me a geometric magazine illustration of a train and a quotation from the poet Edna St. Vincent Millay to adapt for stitchery. I returned to her a simple line drawing on hardanger cloth. Several months later, after a performing tour of Europe, Regina had transformed the primitive drawing into a dazzling piece of needlework. Breaking all the rules of contemporary stitchery, she had tightly packed continental stitches on the hardanger, usually used for cross-stitching. The finished piece, with a glowing surface reminiscent of beading, had so little in common with the drawing I had done that only a detailed chart can adequately describe the stunning color and stitch placement.

Materials Needed

Off-white hardanger cloth, 22 threads to the inch, 14″×14″, edges basted or taped
※8 DMC pearl cotton, 1 ball in each of the following colors:
  navy blue ※823
  medium blue ※796
  light blue ※827
  cranberry ※902
  red ※498
  salmon ※353
  yellow ※745
  black ※310
  brown ※434
  beige ※642
  slate gray ※318
  light green ※368
  green ※904
Embroidery needle
Scissors
Graph paper and pencil
Embroidery hoop

TRAIN SAMPLER (PART 1).

Color key for Train Sampler:

- NAVY BLUE
- LIGHT BLUE
- MEDIUM BLUE
- CRANBERRY
- RED
- SALMON
- YELLOW
- BLACK
- BEIGE
- SLATE GRAY
- BROWN
- LIGHT GREEN
- GREEN

TRAIN SAMPLER (PART 2).

Unusual Characteristics

The chart given shows only the left side of the train and smoke to be stitched. Copy it on each side, reversing the design for the right-hand side, for a symmetrical look. The smoke areas in the actual sampler are irregular, so allow yourself to improvise, making each side different, if you like.

Be sure to use a hoop when working on this piece and pull your stitches as gently as possible to help minimize fabric distortion. Even with these precautions, however, you may find that your fabric has puckered. Block your embroidery back into shape as described on page 42.

Preparation

Chart your initials on graph paper for use in sampler and mark with centering lines. On fabric, put in basting lines for centering, as shown on page 22.

Procedure

Step 1

Using the accompanying chart and your own graphed initials, begin stitching in the center of the sampler and work outward. Use a single strand of pearl cotton over a single mesh (2 grouped threads) of hardanger cloth to make continental stitches, as shown on page 38. There are approximately 22 stitches per inch.

Step 2

When stitching is complete, block embroidery as needed, mount, and frame. Finishing instructions are in Chapter Six, "Finishing Needlework."

CROSS-STITCH BABY SAMPLER ON SUPERFINE LINEN

Finished size: 19″×28″ (plus frame)

Ann Lloyd's spectacular baby sampler, stitched for her daughter Susan, is truly a family heirloom. The background linen, which was dipped in tea to give it a subtle color, is from a sheet that had belonged to Ann's husband's grandmother.

Ann Lloyd planned her own design first on graph paper, using cross-stitch pattern books and her own original motifs. This sampler, which is her first, took two and a half years to complete, as shown by the dates 1954 to 1956 marked on the lower right-hand corner of the stitchery. She has, however, gone on to create other samplers of similar complexity in much less time. Also pictured in the photograph is an in-progress sampler with the scrim basted to the superfine linen.

Color key for Cross-stitch Baby Sampler on Superfine Linen:

Ⓐ	AQUA
☒	DARK GREEN
⊞	BROWN
ⓑ	DARK BLUE
ⓑ	BLUE
Ⓡ	RED
Ⓟ	PINK
Ⓟ	DARK PINK
Ⓨ	YELLOW
Ⓨ	DARK YELLOW
⊿	MINT GREEN
⊠	GREEN
Ⓛ	LAVENDER
ⓗ	OFF-WHITE
ⓒ	OCHER
◍	DARK GRAY
Ⓞ	GRAY
ⓝ	ORANGE

CROSS-STITCH BABY SAMPLER ON SUPERFINE LINEN (PART 1).

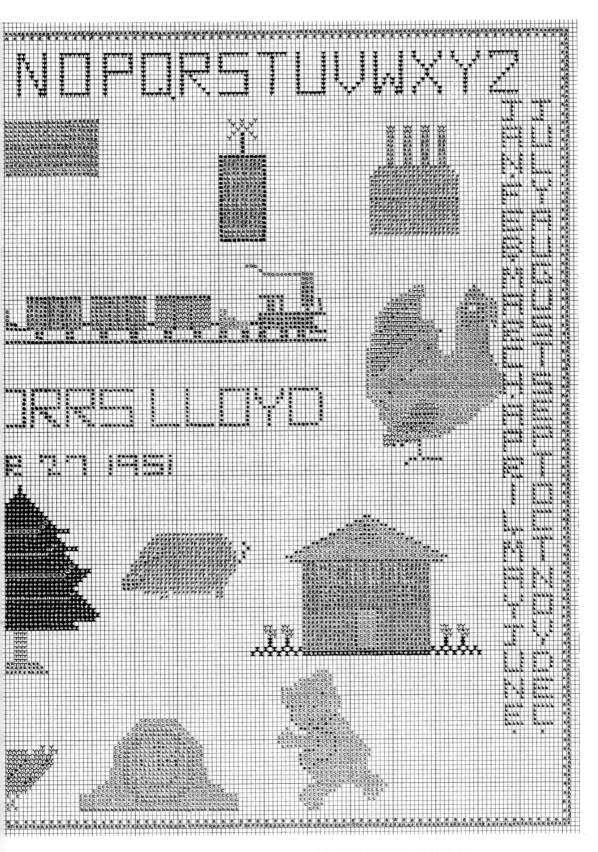

CROSS-STITCH BABY SAMPLER ON SUPERFINE LINEN (PART 2).

CROSS-STITCH SAMPLER ON SUPERFINE LINEN IN PROGRESS.

Materials Needed

Fine linen sheeting, 19"×28" or size appropriate to your project, plus
   ample seam allowance, edges basted or taped
Scrim or waste mesh, 10 threads per inch, cut to the same size
6-strand embroidery floss, 1 skein of each of the following colors:

black	dark blue	mint green
brown	dark pink	green
gray	dark green	ocher
pink	off-white	lavender
blue	orange	dark yellow
aqua	yellow	dark gray
red		

Wise Old Owl Sampler.

Quick Point Sampler Rug.

Knit Baby Overalls, Sampler Baby Bib, Sampler Baby Sweater.

Sampler Tote.

Family Sampler.

Needlepoint Sampler Belt.

Family Sampler: detail.

Cross-stitch Baby Sampler on Superfine
Linen.

Train Sampler.

Train Sampler: detail.

Needlepoint House Sampler Pillow.

Gingham Sampler Quilt.

Needlepoint House Sampler Pillow: detail.

Sampler Birthday Pillow.

Dish Towel Sampler.

1831 Sampler.

Hardanger Baby Sampler.

Sampler with Cotton Thread.

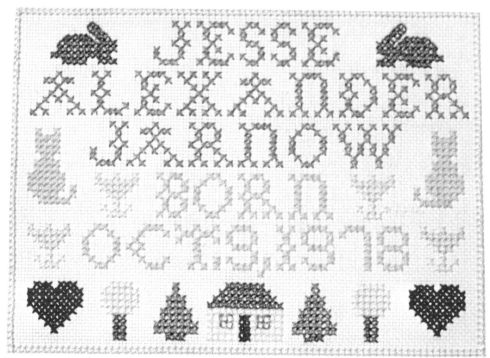

Hardanger Baby Sampler: detail.

Sampler with Cotton Thread: detail.

New York City Sampler.

New York City Sampler: detail.

Grandma Pillow.

Yellow Cat Pillow.

Stencil Birthday Pillow and Stencil Alphabet Pillow.

Embroidery needle
Small, pointed scissors
Tweezers
Graph paper and pencil
Embroidery hoop
Basting thread (2 colors)

Unusual Characteristics

Since the threads of linen sheeting are too fine to count, apply scrim or waste mesh to the surface of the linen with basting stitches. Purchase it at a needlework specialty shop in your area or order it from the sources on page 4. As you work your cross-stitches, pull them tighter than usual so they will sit flat when the mesh is removed.

Remove the mesh only when all stitching is complete. To do this, cut the mesh carefully with small, pointed scissors and use tweezers to pull out the strands one at a time. Pull gently to avoid disturbing the stitchery. It is slow, painstaking work.

Preparation

On superfine linen, graph out the name and birth date you wish to include in your sampler, using the alphabet shown in the chart for this sampler. Adjust the dimensions of the background fabric according to your needs.

Tint linen sheeting for an antique look, if you like, by soaking it in tea until it reaches the desired shade. Remember that fabric will dry slightly lighter. Be sure to rinse fabric thoroughly before beginning stitchery. Allow fabric to dry, and then press.

Cut both linen for embroidery and scrim or waste mesh to the same size. Center and smooth scrim over face of linen sheeting and baste securely together.

Mark center lines of scrim with basting lines as described on page 22. Use a thread color that is distinguishable from previous basting.

Procedure

Step 1

Begin to cross-stitch the name and birth date in the center of sampler, as described on page 23. Cover 2 threads of the scrim at a time, using 2 strands of floss. Be sure your stitching goes between the threads of the scrim, not through them. It must, however, go through the linen sheeting. Use an embroidery hoop to help keep your stitches even.

Step 2

When lettering is complete, add other motifs as shown on chart, or any others, as desired.

Step 3

When all stitching is complete, including your own signature or initials, remove basting stitches and threads of scrim, as described above.

Step 4

Finishing instructions are in Chapter Six, "Finishing Needlework."

Iron completed embroidery with care. Mount and frame, as described on page 53.

1831 SAMPLER

Finished size: 12"×14" (plus frame)

The 1831 Sampler, purchased in New Orleans in its original simulated rosewood frame, has been hanging in my cousins' home for several years. Although I had looked at it often, it wasn't until I borrowed it for charting and photographing that I discovered its startling inconsistencies. Many old samplers are stitched without the letter *J,* as an economy. This sampler is also missing a *G* and a *Y* within the script alphabet—certainly oversights.

This is an inviting sampler for today's needleworkers to copy because its charming borders and alphabets are cross-stitched on a large uncovered background fabric similar to today's needlepoint penelope canvas.

Materials Needed

Natural-color penelope mesh, 12 threads to the inch, approximately 14"×16", edges taped
Persian needlepoint yarn, in the following colors, ½ ounce each, except where noted (be sure to keep your selections muted):
    light gray-green
    dark gray-green
    red
    apricot
    yellow
    blue
    black
    olive green (1 yard)
Tapestry needle
Scissors
Graph paper and pencil
Needlepoint frame (optional)

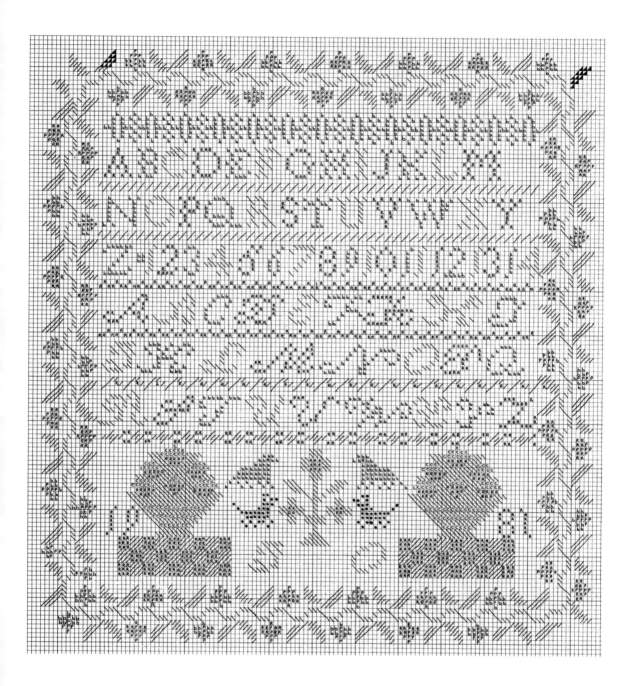

1831 SAMPLER.

Unusual Characteristics

The chart given here has been amended slightly to include the missing letters and to allow room for a signature. The original has only two initials stitched in the center, near the bottom. In addition, some of the script letters, which are illegible, have been clarified. Make any additional adaptations that seem appropriate, but to maintain the antique look, don't let the design arrangement become too perfect.

Preparation

Using one of the alphabets shown on the 1831 chart, mark out your name and the date on graph paper. Plan to center this information in the open space given in the chart. If you wish to rearrange the design in any way, do this on graph paper first before you begin to stitch. Allow for any additional rows of stitching you have planned before cutting the canvas.

Put in basting lines down and across the center axes to facilitate centering. Centering information is on page 22.

Color key for 1831 Sampler:

P	APRICOT
b	BLUE
R	RED
c	YELLOW
☐	LIGHT GRAY-GREEN
◢	OLIVE GREEN
☒	DARK GRAY-GREEN
●	BLACK

Procedure

Step 1

Following the chart given and your own additions, begin to cross-stitch in the center of the canvas. Use 3 strands of Persian yarn to cover each double thread of penelope mesh. To avoid canvas distortion, use a needlepoint frame.

Step 2

Complete the design, using cross-stitches, but do not cover background canvas with stitchery.

Step 3

Block and finish, according to the instructions which begin on page 42. Mount and frame, as described on page 53.

SAMPLER WITH COTTON THREAD

Finished size: 16"×12¾"

When Dorothy Twining Globus saw the small skeins of cotton Retors à Broder embroidery thread in a flea market, she was attracted to the soft muted colors and textures. She bought an assortment of colors without a specific project in mind and soon used it to create a sampler for her new son, Sam, whose initials are stitched into the design. The dates shown at the bottom of the stitchery are the years the sampler was begun and finished. In addition, there are two nearly empty boxes to each side of these dates which are ideal for your own name or initials and location.

Materials Needed

Aida cloth, 12 threads to the inch, 16"×12¾", plus ample seam allowance, edges basted or taped

Retors à Broder thread in colors shown on the chart (this thread is available from the sources listed on page 4)

Tapestry needle

Embroidery hoop

Graph paper and pencil

Unusual Characteristics

Since only half of each row of stitchery is shown in the accompanying chart, be sure to stitch the second half of each line for a complete sampler.

Because this is an intricate and personal sampler, you may find it difficult to duplicate exactly. Instead, study the photograph in the color section and use the stitch chart as inspiration for your own sampler. You will find it especially difficult to duplicate the sunset motif, which is a particularly free-form design. Follow the photograph closely and refer to the chart for guidance.

Preparation

Put in basting lines to mark the center and outside dimensions of the sampler as shown on page 22.

Chart on graph paper the information you wish to include in your sampler, using the alphabet shown on page 18.

Procedure

Step 1

Using the accompanying chart, begin in the center of the sampler and stitch toward an outer edge. Use the standard 6 strands of thread with a tapestry needle and an embroidery hoop. Stitch until one row is complete.

Step 2

Continue stitching in lines of pattern until the sampler is complete. Be sure to add your own initials, where appropriate.

Finishing

Although the background cloth may pucker as you work, this can be easily corrected by blocking. Do this at home, according to the instructions given on page 42. Mount and frame the sampler for display, as described on page 53, or have all finishing work done in a local reputable needlework or frame shop.

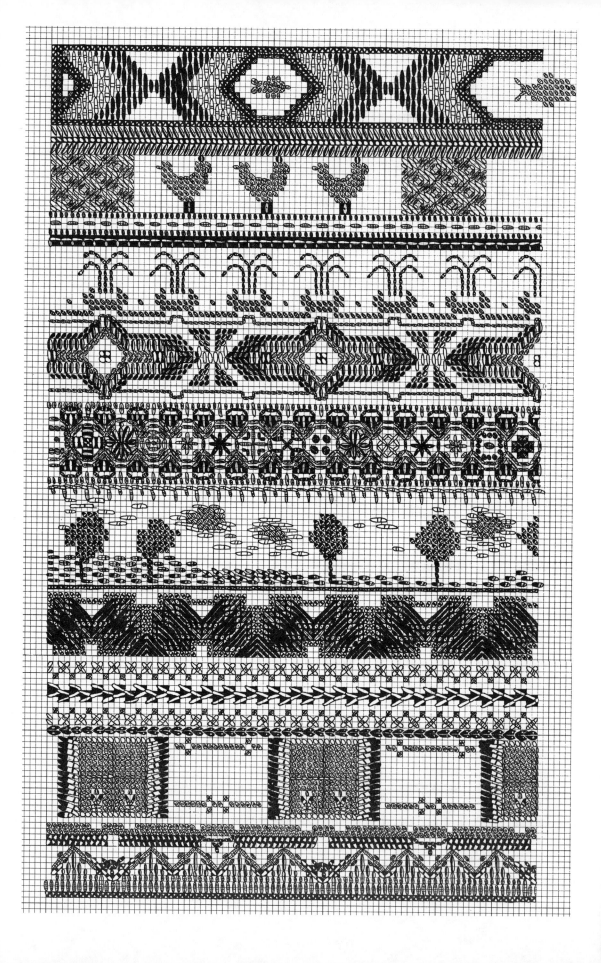

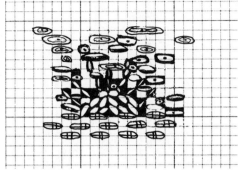

Sunset motif

Color key for Sampler with Cotton Thread and sunset motif:

◨	▭	DARK YELLOW
◳	▱	LIGHT YELLOW
◣	⬬	GRAY
◍	◫	SKY BLUE
◈	◫	BLUE
◪	◫	DARK BLUE
◙	◫	NAVY BLUE
◩	◧	PINK
◖	◗	CRANBERRY
◐	◫	FUCHSIA
◍	◔	BEIGE
◉	◎	LAVENDER
◩		CREAM
◉	◕	GOLD
◉	◒	LIGHT BROWN
◨	◕	DARK BROWN
◧	◧	COPPER
◙	◪	DARK COPPER
◐	◖	GREEN
◉	◫	LIGHT GREEN
◍	◫	APPLE GREEN
◪	◫	DARK APPLE GREEN
◍	◫	GRAY-GREEN

SAMPLER WITH COTTON THREAD—left half only.

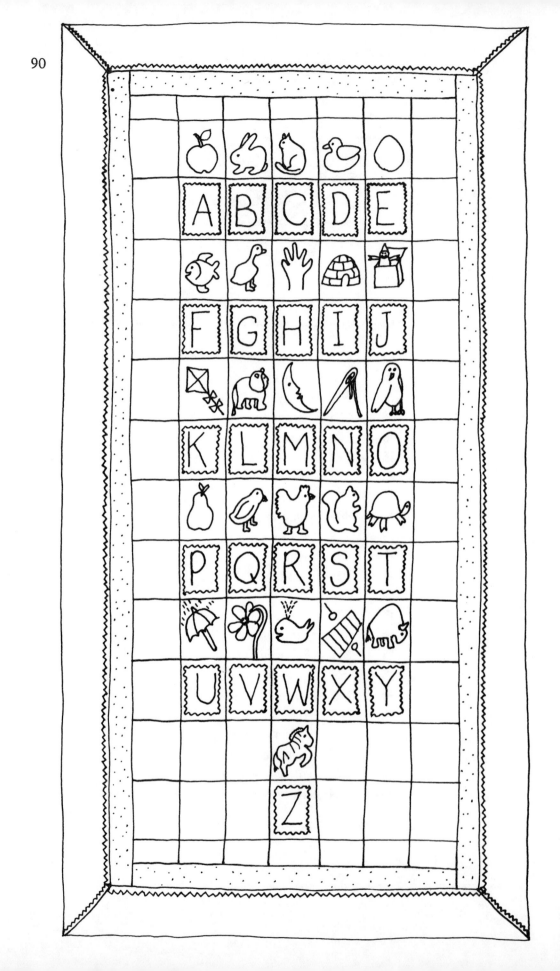

DISH TOWEL SAMPLER

Finished size: 20″×33½″ (including added fabric borders)

Who could resist the ready-made grid of a woven linen dish towel? It was just begging to be filled with a cross-stitch alphabet and simple stem stitch pictures. The decorative borders around each letter are variations woven into a backstitched frame. The finished quilt, perfectly sized for a newborn baby, is also an eye-catching decoration for a child's room.

After the embroidery is complete, add decorative fabrics, quilt filling, and backing. Sew several small plastic rings across the back near the top edge of the quilt and suspend from a row of firmly attached nails in the wall.

Materials Needed

1 white dish towel with horizontal and vertical lines woven in blue, measuring 19½″×29½″ (this one contains 7 boxes marked across and 12 running the length of the towel; it was purchased at B. Altman & Co., New York City, through the housewares catalog)

⚹5 DMC pearl cotton, 2 skeins of each of the following colors:
scarlet ⚹350
teal blue ⚹517
bright yellow ⚹444
orange ⚹740

For inner patchwork border:
2 strips fabric, each 14½″×¾″, plus seam allowance
2 strips fabric, each 28″×¾″, plus seam allowance

For backing and outer border:
1 piece fabric, 38½″×25″, plus seam allowance
Quilt batting or flannel lining, 20″×33½″, plus seam allowance (optional)

Embroidery needle
Scissors
Graph paper and pencil
Embroidery hoop

DISH TOWEL SAMPLER.

Unusual Characteristics

When you inspect the dish towel, you will discover that the vertical threads are doubled. Treat these verticals as a single thread when doing stitchery. Since the threads are so closely woven, this will not be difficult. Letters stitched into this fabric will appear flatter than the model shown in the chart because of the weave, a quality that should be accepted as the nature of the material.

The *M* has been made narrower, as shown, to fit more comfortably into the design.

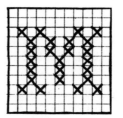

Compact M for Dish Towel Sampler.

Procedure

Step 1

Enlarge and transfer drawings to appropriate boxes, as shown in accompanying illustrations.

Step 2

Using stem stitch and backstitch, embroider over picture outlines, using mostly scarlet thread. For highlights, use a small amount of blue stitching in areas such as the animals' eyes and the stems of fruit.

Step 3

Beginning in the first box of row 2, put in embroidered borders (which will surround the letters). Each border is based on the same double row of broken backstitches, as shown, which are done in scarlet and orange alternately. Although each border is improvised, the basic colors are scarlet, orange, and bright yellow. Blue is used only as a highlight.

Step 4

Weave threads through backstitches, as shown. Here are some suggested variations, although you may enjoy inventing some of your own. For further ideas, study other stitches shown in this book.

Step 5

Add blue stitching to the borders, as either woven threads, vertical straight stitches, or french knots.

Step 6

Embroider the remaining 25 borders in alternate rows, with the last (letter Z) centered at the bottom, as shown in the drawing of the completed sampler.

Step 7

Using the traditional cross-stitch alphabet shown on page 17, put in the alphabet in orange and scarlet, alternating. Cross-stitches cover 4 horizontal threads and 4 doubled vertical threads. Be sure to see "Unusual Characteristics" above.

Step 8

Using graph paper, chart your own initials, the date, and your location, abbreviated. Stitch these so that the initials and date are flush with the right edge and the location is flush with the left. Cross-stitches cover only 2 threads, and letters are half the size of the alphabet in the main part of the sampler.

Step 9

Finish the sampler as a quilt or wall hanging by adding inner patchwork border strips and quilt lining and backing, as shown on page 50.

MOTIFS TO EMBROIDER FOR DISH TOWEL SAMPLER.

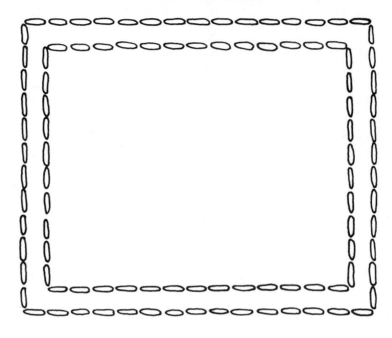

BORDERS FOR DISH TOWEL SAMPLER.

Improvise borders. First put in backstitch foundation, as shown. Count threads for even stitch placement. Then weave threads and add straight stitches and french knots. Shown are 4 different suggested motifs.

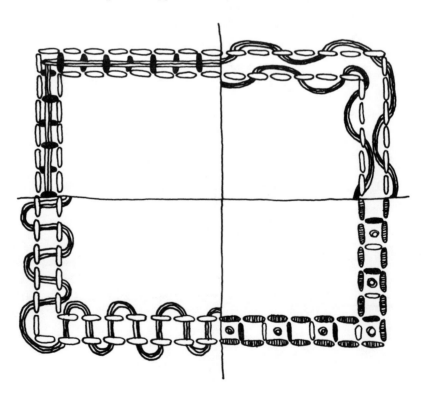

WISE OLD OWL SAMPLER

Finished size: 10½"×12½" (plus seam allowance)

After looking at books of historic needlework, I wanted to create my own stitchery with a timeless, intricate appearance. Using an 1870 quotation from *Punch,* an English humor magazine, and a drawing that I developed from a photograph of an owl, I refined my design.

Finding the appropriate fabric became an unexpected problem. I needed a natural linen with a weave large enough for counted-thread cross-stitch but small enough for delicate embroidery. Finally I found what I needed at The Four Wives in Cold Spring Harbor, New York (see page 4). The natural-color linen with slightly uneven strands has approximately 35 threads per inch. Doing stitchery at night, even with the aid of a gooseneck lamp, was too much of a strain for my eyes. Strong, shaded daylight was the only light I found comfortable for stitching. Even then, progress was slower than I ever would have imagined.

Materials Needed

Natural-color linen, with approximately 35 threads to the inch horizontally
  (fewer vertically), 15"×18", edges basted or taped
※25 DMC 6-strand embroidery floss, 1 skein for each color, except where
  noted:
  pink ※950
  rose ※407
  maroon ※221
  light green ※3053
  yellow-green ※3013
  dark blue-green ※924
  light brown ※644 (2 skeins)
  dark brown ※938
  brown ※3021
  palest yellow ※746
  pale yellow ※3078
  yellow ※727
  ocher ※3045
  terra-cotta ※632
  gray ※762
  black ※310
Embroidery needle (size 12)
Scissors
Embroidery hoop

Enlarge to 8"

Color Placement

Lettering: maroon, dark blue-green
Signature and *anon:* light green
Tree: outline: brown
   filling: light brown
Acorns: outline: dark brown
   filling: light brown, dark brown, ocher
Leaves: outline: dark blue-green
   inner lines: light green, yellow-green
Owl: outline: dark brown
   eyes and feet outline: black
   outer eye: light brown, pink
   inner eye: yellow
   ears: ocher
   feathers: ocher, light brown
   outline below each feather: pink
   chest: ocher, light brown, dark brown
   feet filling: light brown
Grass: top layer: yellow-green
   middle: light green
   bottom: dark blue-green
Squirrel: outline: dark brown
   face: black
   filling: gray
Butterfly: outline: dark brown
   lines on wings: dark brown
   inner body: rose
   outer wings: terra-cotta, dark brown
   inner wings: yellow, rose, palest yellow
Flower leaves: outline: dark blue-green
   filling: light green
Flower outline: maroon
   filling: pink

WISE OLD OWL SAMPLER.

A WISE OLD OWL
SAT IN AN OAK,
THE MORE HE SAW
THE LESS HE SPOKE,
THE LESS HE SPOKE
THE MORE HE HEARD,
WHY CAN'T WE ALL
BE LIKE THAT
WISE OLD BIRD?

ANON

Lettering for Wise Old Owl Sampler.

Unusual Characteristics

The fabric is an uneven-weave linen not usually recommended for counted-thread embroidery. As a result, the lettering, worked over the surface as consistently as possible, takes on a slightly uneven look usually seen in antique samplers. It is a quality not possible with the more popular even-weave fabrics such as hardanger or Aida cloth. Once you become experienced in counted-thread embroidery, you will be better able to choose appropriate offbeat fabrics for your embroidery. For more on even-weave fabric, see page 5.

Procedure

Step 1

Enlarge artwork to appropriate size, as described on page 26 and indicated in the accompanying drawing.

Step 2

Transfer artwork to linen, as described on page 27.

Step 3

Using the cross-stitch, stitch in letters, as shown on chart. Use 2 strands of embroidery floss to cover 1 strand of canvas.

Step 4

Using 2 strands of floss, outline and fill the drawn shapes with simple embroidery stitches: stem stitch, backstitch, satin stitch, and french knots.

Step 5

Add 3 rows of cross-stitching around the outside of the design. Make stitches over 2 threads. The inner row, ocher, is 147 stitches wide and 127 stitches high. The outside borders, pink and maroon, are each 1 stitch longer at each end than the previous row. Because of the uneven fabric structure, the finished result is a rectangle 8½ inches wide and 10½ inches high.

Add your initials and the date, using the alphabet on page 17.

Step 6

Finishing instructions are in Chapter Six, "Finishing Needlework." Mount and frame this sampler with a 1-inch border of fabric visible on all sides.

QUICK POINT SAMPLER RUG

Finished size: 21½″×31″

After working for several weeks on the eye-straining Wise Old Owl (preceding sampler), I was ready for a more whimsical, easygoing project. A roll of quick point needlepoint mesh, which has 5 squares to the inch, caught my eye in The Four Wives needlework shop as I was buying a few skeins of floss to finish up the Wise Old Owl. A quick point rug seemed like the perfect follow-up project. In terms of hours spent stitching, the rug probably took as much time to complete as the Wise Old Owl Sampler, but the ease with which I was able to stitch made the rug seem to go infinitely faster.

Materials Needed

Quick point mesh, 5 squares to the inch, 28″×38″, edges bound with basted fabric or tape (do *not* use 4-to-the-inch latch-hook canvas, as fine Persian yarn will not cover it adequately)

Persian needlepoint yarn, in the following colors, 1 ounce each except where noted (the numbers given are for Paternayan yarn; see page 4 for shops that carry it)

Color key for Quick Point Sampler Rug:

[L]	LAVENDER
[O]	BLUE
⧄	MINT GREEN
[Y]	PALE YELLOW
[R]	APRICOT
⧐	SCARLET
⊞	OFF-WHITE
[n]	SALMON
[b]	BEIGE
⊠	GRAY-GREEN

     apricot ✳982
     gray-green ✳756
     pale yellow ✳437
     scarlet ✳238
     lavender ✳620
     beige ✳136
     mint green ✳535
     off-white ✳012
     blue ✳743
     salmon ✳982
     deep blue ✳365 (outer background—18 ounces)
     dark green ✳402 (alphabet background—4 ounces)
Tapestry needle
Scissors
Frame (optional)
Graph paper and pencil
Cobalt-blue acrylic paint (optional)
Small paintbrush (optional)
Dish (optional)
Heavy-duty hand sewing thread and needle (optional)
Cotton rug binding, 2″ wide, 3½ yards (optional)

Unusual Characteristics

Quick point has a few special technical problems of its own that are worth mentioning. First, be sure to weave the beginning and end of each strand you stitch with particular care. I didn't. The result was that much of my foreground stitching loosened or came undone as I worked, and it needed to be restitched—not always a simple matter.

You may want to work this rug on a frame. Again, I didn't, and the resulting rug, after intense blocking, is still not perfectly rectangular. Check your local needlework shop for supplies.

When working, do not pull your yarn too tightly. This will lessen the distortion and help prevent the backing mesh from showing through.

In addition, 6 strands of the dark blue and dark green wool used for the background stitching did not cover the mesh adequately and I had to add an extra 2 strands to each threading. This was also true of the lavender.

Even with the extra strands of yarn, the white rug mesh was still visible behind the deep blue background stitching. Yet if I had added more strands of yarn, my stitching would have been too tight, puckering the mesh. You can avoid this dilemma by carefully covering the threads of the mesh *before* you begin needlework with watered-down cobalt-blue acrylic paint, applied with a soft paintbrush. If you are planning to use another dark color for the background, choose acrylic paint to match. Use only acrylic paint, which is completely waterproof when dry. Thin the paint with water to a wash consistency to prevent excess paint from chipping off and becoming entangled in your yarn. Do all the painting and allow the paint to dry thoroughly before you begin your stitchery. I was not able to use this procedure because I didn't decide on the color of the background until all the other stitching was complete.

Preparation

Using the alphabet shown on the chart with this sampler, mark out your name and the date on graph paper. Plan to center this information in the appropriate space on the sampler, as described on page 22. Abbreviate names or use initials as needed. If you wish to add more lettering than space allows, enlarge the boxed alphabet area, using graph paper. The canvas size given can accommodate only one more row of lettering, so if your needs extend beyond this, plan to use a longer canvas.

Procedure

Step 1

Following the chart, begin to stitch in the center of the canvas. Put in the alphabet, your name and date, and the double border outlines, using the continental stitch with 6 strands of yarn.

Step 2

Put in background stitching, using 8 strands of dark green yarn. Use the basketweave stitch as much as possible. Filling in this area can be difficult because the lettering is scattered and broken.

Step 3

Returning to the center of the chart and canvas, put in the children, cats, birds, flowers, outline borders, and all other foreground shapes, using the continental stitch and 6 strands of yarn. Use 8 strands of lavender yarn or of any other color if that color seems too thin.

Step 4

When all foreground shapes have been added, put in the background, using the basketweave stitch and 8 strands of dark blue yarn.

Step 5

Embroider cats' whiskers over the finished needlepoint by couching single strands of off-white yarn. Make a ¾″ straight stitch for each whisker and secure each length with 3 tiny crosswise stitches, as shown.

Couching cat's whiskers over needlepoint.

Step 6

Block the completed rug according to the instructions on page 42. Turn under the edges and cover with cotton rug binding. For a wall hanging, sew plastic rings across the top and hang on nails on a wall.

GRANDMA PILLOW

Finished size: 14½″×11¾″ (plus 2″ ruffle)

How could a sampler collection be complete without the most famous maxim of all? "There's no place like home . . . except Grandma's" is an amended version that a lot of people will find fun and meaningful.

This sophisticated yet easy-to-make pillow was created by Betsy Potter as a present for her mother, a perfect accent for her red, white, and blue living room. The central panel is needlepoint, and the outer borders are strips of printed cotton. You can easily adapt the colors for your own decorating needs, but for the same charming effect as the one shown, be sure to combine small polka dots, flowers, and a gingham ruffle in the colors of your choice for your finished pillow.

Materials Needed

For needlepoint panel:
Mono mesh, 12 threads to the inch, 8″×5¼″, plus adequate seam allowance, edges taped
Persian needlepoint yarn in the following colors:
    off-white (1 ounce)
    navy blue (½ ounce)
    red (¼ ounce)
    yellow (1 length—1 yard)
Tapestry needle
Small scissors
For patchwork panels:
    2 pieces polka-dot fabric, each 8″×2″, plus seam allowance
    2 pieces polka-dot fabric, each 2″×9¼″, plus seam allowance
    2 pieces flowered fabric, each 1¼″×9¼″, plus seam allowance
    2 pieces flowered fabric, each 14½″×1½″, plus seam allowance
Gingham for ruffle, 2½ yards (pieced if needed), 2″ wide, one edge turned and hemmed
Denim for pillow back, 14½″×12¼″, plus seam allowance
Hand sewing thread and needle
Straight pins
Iron
Sewing machine
Dacron polyester fiberfill, 12-ounce bag

Procedure: Needlepoint Panel

Step 1

Following the accompanying chart, complete the lettering in navy blue and the decorative motifs in red and yellow. Use the continental stitch, shown on page 38.

Step 2

Fill in background, using continental or basketweave stitch.

Step 3

Block according to instructions on page 42.

Color key for Grandma Pillow:

☒ NAVY BLUE

ℝ RED

𝕐 YELLOW

Procedure: Patchwork Panels

Step 1

Cut out all materials and set aside.

Step 2

Attach patchwork borders in the order indicated in the accompanying illustration. Treat the completed needlepoint as if it were any other fabric. Pin a polka-dot fabric strip (8″×2″) to the needlepoint, face to face, and machine-stitch down one edge. Remove pins and press with iron.

Step 3

When top and bottom strips are stitched in position, attach polka-dot fabric strips to the sides of the needlepoint, using the same method. Remove pins and press.

Step 4

Add shorter flowered fabric strips to the sides, using the same method.

Step 5

Attach the top and bottom flowered strips, using the same method.

Step 6

When all border strips are attached, press again with hot iron.

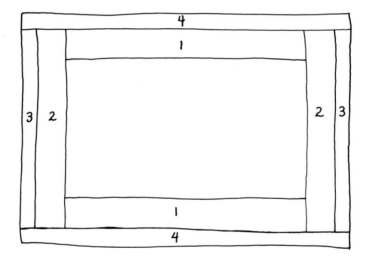

Adding a double patchwork border.
(*For more on patchwork borders, see the drawing on page 160.*)

Procedure: Ruffled Edge

Step 1

Gather the gingham fabric (in the amount described in materials list) into soft ruffles and pin around the outside edge on the face of the completed pillow top, as shown in the illustration.

Step 2

Stitch in place. Remove pins. Check for correct position of ruffle.

Step 3

Fold ruffle back over pillow face and repin to prevent ruffle from becoming caught in pillow construction, which follows.

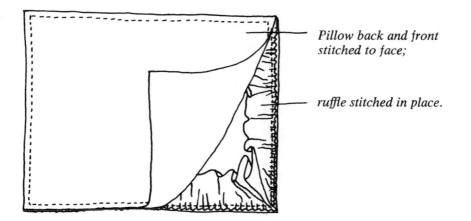

Pillow back and front stitched to face;

ruffle stitched in place.

Pillow Construction

Step 1

Pin completed pillow face, including ruffle, face to face with denim pillow back.

Step 2

Machine-stitch around all sides ¼″ from outside edge, leaving a 6″ opening on the bottom for reversing the pillow. Remove pins.

Step 3

Turn pillow right side out. Remove all ruffle pins.

Step 4

Stuff with Dacron polyester fiberfill. Turn under remaining hem and hand-stitch closed.

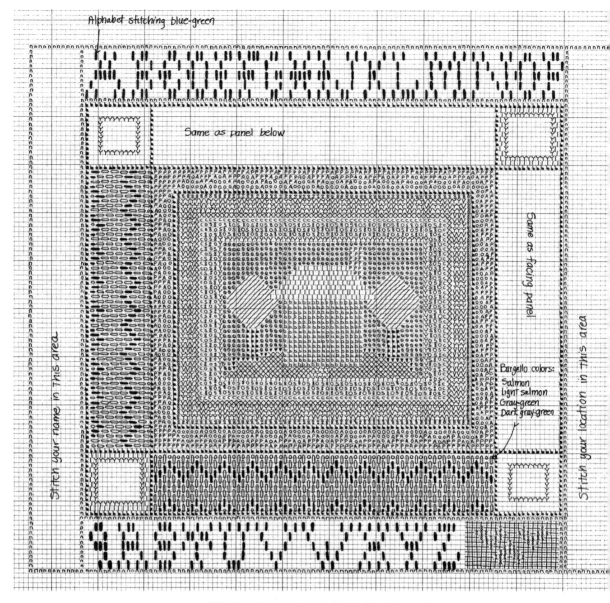

NEEDLEPOINT HOUSE SAMPLER PILLOW.

Color key for Needlepoint House Sampler Pillow:

◘	LIGHT BLUE	ℙ	APRICOT
◙	MEDIUM BLUE	Ⓨ	YELLOW
●	BLUE-GREEN	ⓢ	LIGHT SALMON
◩	LIGHT GRAY-GREEN	⑧	SALMON
⊠	DARK GRAY-GREEN	ⓑ	LIGHT BROWN
Ⓐ	APPLE GREEN	Ⅱ	BROWN
Ⓥ	LIGHT OLIVE	ⓑ	DARK BROWN
▼	OLIVE	ⓝ	PINK
ⓒ	OCHER	⊞	GRAY-GREEN

NEEDLEPOINT HOUSE SAMPLER PILLOW

Finished size: 13½″×11½″

The delicately colored Needlepoint House Sampler Pillow is a combination of continental and bargello stitches, with touches of embroidery added on top for extra dimension. Before beginning to stitch, be sure to chart out your own name, date, and location, using the alphabet from the top and bottom panel as shown in the chart on page 17. Make any necessary adjustments to accommodate your needs.

The yarn I used for this pillow was left over from other needlepoint projects. If you are an active needlepointer, you may want to make color changes with leftovers of your own, so that the finished pillow will blend well with your other needlepoint projects.

Materials Needed

Mono mesh, 10 threads to the inch, 16″×14″, with edges taped
Tapestry needle
Scissors
Graph paper and pencil
Good-quality Persian yarn, ½ ounce of each of the following colors,
    except where noted:
    pink (1 ounce)
    light blue
    medium blue
    light gray-green
    gray-green
    dark gray-green
    apple green
    light olive
    olive
    ocher
    apricot
    yellow
    light salmon
    salmon
    light brown
    brown
    dark brown
    blue-green

Velvet for pillow back, 13½″×11½″, plus seam allowance
Straight pins
Dacron polyester fiberfill, 12-ounce bag
Sewing machine
Hand sewing thread and needle

Unusual Characteristics

The lettering shown in the chart for this sampler is done with an upright satin stitch, known in needlepoint as gobelin. For greater legibility, consider using the continental stitch instead, covering the same threads indicated in the chart.

Preparation

Using the alphabet shown in the accompanying chart, chart out your name and location on graph paper. There are 108 spaces within each side panel as the design now stands. Count the spaces you will need for your information, including the spaces between the words. Abbreviate the date and location if necessary. If the information you wish to include still will not fit, add a compatible bargello stripe on the top and the bottom of the design, which will lengthen the side panels.

Procedure

Step 1

Following the accompanying chart, begin in the center. Use 2 strands of yarn in your needle for all work except where noted. Put in all frame lines, using the continental stitch:

> pale yellow
> ocher
> dark gray-green
> salmon
> dark brown (3 times)

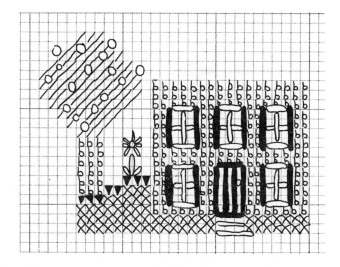

House detail showing placement of straight stitches and french knots. Darkened straight stitches are blue-green. French knots, indicated by circles, are pink and light olive. All other colors are shown in key.

NEEDLEPOINT HOUSE DETAILS.

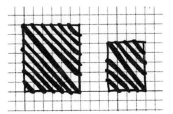

Corner details are done in straight stitches; stitch central areas on the diagonal, as shown.

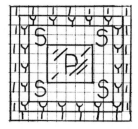 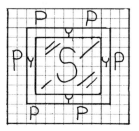

To complete corners, first make rectangular frames using the continental stitch, following the color placement indicated.

Step 2

Using the continental stitch, put in the house, sky, trees, and grass.

Working into the finished needlepoint, add french knots in the trees, flowers, and doorknob. Use 3 strands of yarn for all french knots (shown on page 37), except *one* strand for blue-green. Using single strands of wool, add window frames and shutters, door and doorstep, and flower stems.

Step 3

Using the continental stitch, and working outward, put in the 3 geometric patterns shown in the chart.

Step 4

Using straight stitch, put in bargello pattern on all 4 sides, including corner patterns, as shown. Make stitches over 2 threads of mesh.

Step 5

Using straight stitches, put in the alphabet on the top and bottom panels.

Step 6

Put in your name, location, and date on the side panels.

Step 7

Using straight stitches, put in the background behind the letters.

Step 8

Add 3 rows of continental stitch on all sides in dark brown, to be used as seam allowance in pillow construction.

Step 9

Block according to instructions on page 42. Stitch into knife-edge pillow, as described on page 47.

———————————

SAMPLER BIRTHDAY PILLOW

Finished size: 15"×15"

This gingham patchwork birthday pillow is a delightful gift that will remind the recipient of his or her special day throughout the year. Although this pillow looks especially nice with the Gingham Sampler Quilt on page 129, it can add good cheer to any bed, chair, or sofa.

This project is ideal for a beginner. The cross-stitching, made simple by the large gingham grid, can be completed in a few sittings. With the aid of a sewing machine, the pillow itself can be assembled in less than an hour.

SAMPLER BIRTHDAY PILLOW.

Materials Needed

4 squares of gingham, 8 boxes per inch, 5¾″×5¾″—2 squares of turquoise and white, 2 squares of lime green and white

2 strips printed fabric, each 10½″×2¼″, plus seam allowance, for borders

2 strips printed fabric, each 15″×2¼″, plus seam allowance, for borders

1 piece printed fabric, 15″×15″, plus seam allowance, for pillow back

6-strand embroidery floss, 1 skein of each of the following colors:

    dark green
    light green
    yellow
    dark yellow
    white
    pink
    brown
    turquoise
    salmon

1 package jumbo yellow rickrack

Dacron polyester fiberfill, 12-ounce bag

Graph paper and pencil

Straight pins

Embroidery needle

Scissors

Iron

Sewing machine

Hand sewing thread and needle

Unusual Characteristics

If gingham with 8 boxes per inch is not available, choose the next closest size, but adjust the finished size of the pillow accordingly. If you follow the directions given, using gingham with smaller squares (and more boxes per inch) you will create a smaller pillow. Gingham with larger squares and less boxes per inch will give you a larger, more elementary pillow. To cross-stitch in larger squares, add an additional strand of floss in your needle. Remove a strand for more delicate gingham, as needed.

Preparation

Iron all fabrics.

Charts for Sampler Birthday Pillow.

Color key for Sampler Birthday Pillow:

▼	DARK YELLOW	◉	TURQUOISE
⍦	YELLOW	⊙	BLUE
b	BROWN	⌒	WHITE
⊠	DARK GREEN	⑤	SALMON
⧄	LIGHT GREEN	℗	PINK

Procedure

Step 1

Chart name and birthday on graph paper, using the simple cross-stitch alphabet on page 18. If desired, chart your signature on graph paper, using the backstitch alphabet on page 19. Stitch this under the duck motif.

Step 2

Mark centering lines on designs and fabrics, according to the procedure on page 22.

Step 3

Complete stitchery on gingham fabric squares, according to the charts you have planned and the graphs accompanying this project. Use 3 strands of embroidery floss to make one cross-stitch per box of gingham.

Step 4

When all 4 designs are complete, join squares together. To do this, lay out squares face up in correct final position. Place 2 adjoining boxes face to face, pin, and stitch down right-hand side seam, ¼ " from edge. Remove pins, press open, and replace in correct layout. Join 2 additional squares, using the same technique. When stitching is complete, place the 2 stitched strips face to face, pin, and stitch together along top edge. Open and press. This is the central patchwork panel.

Step 5

Place jumbo yellow rickrack down the face of one seam of patchwork panel. Pin and stitch in position. Place rickrack down the face of perpendicular seam. Pin and stitch.

Step 6

Place the completed central patchwork panel on flat surface, face up, with border strips in correct position around it. Join 10½"×2¼" fabric strips to top and bottom of completed patchwork, using the technique described in step 4.

Step 7

Stitch 15″×2¼″ strips to the sides of the patchwork panel, using the same technique. When all stitching is complete, remove pins, open, and press.

Step 8

Place completed pillow front face to face with pillow back. Pin securely and stitch ¼″ from edges on all sides. Leave 3-inch opening in the center of bottom edge for reversing the pillow.

Step 9

When stitching is complete, remove pins, trim corners on the diagonal, and reverse pillow. Gently push out corners with crochet hook or other blunt instrument. Stuff pillow to desired fullness with Dacron polyester fiberfill. Hand-stitch to close bottom seam. For more on pillow construction, see page 45.

Laying out fabric for patchwork.

SAMPLER TOTE.

SAMPLER TOTE

Finished size: 15¼"×17" (*plus seam allowance*)

A personalized tote bag is always a great gift. I made this one for my sister-in-law, Betsy.

For a more rugged tote, consider using blue denim, combining standard blue with navy-blue and white engineer stripes. Use discarded dungarees from your own wardrobe or from a thrift shop, but be sure to use the strong areas of fabric only. Or you can buy denim by the yard in a fabric shop. Because denim is so strong, it won't be necessary to use double layers of fabric, as described in the procedure that follows.

Materials Needed

Natural-color even-weave linen, approximately 10 threads to the inch,
   5″×9″ (adjust these measurements, as explained below; fabric shown is
   available from Boutique Margot, listed on page 4)
For inner patchwork border:
   2 strips beige flowered cotton, each 2½″×8″, plus seam allowance
   2 strips beige flowered cotton, each 2½″×9¼″, plus seam allowance
For tote lining:
   2 pieces beige flowered cotton, each 15¼″×17″, plus seam allowance
For outer patchwork border:
   2 strips green flowered cotton, each 15¼″×2″, plus seam allowance
   2 strips green flowered cotton, each 13″×3″, plus seam allowance
For tote back:
   1 piece green flowered cotton, 15¼″×17″, plus seam allowance
For tote handles:
   4 strips green flowered cotton, 25″×1½″, plus seam allowance (to be
   used doubled)
⅊5 DMC pearl cotton, 1 ball in each of the following colors:
   salmon ⅊352
   light green ⅊913
   dark green ⅊909
   blue ⅊517
Sewing machine
Straight pins
Yardstick
Pencil or chalk
Scissors
Iron
Embroidery hoop (optional)

Unusual Characteristics

The finished Betsy name panel is 8″×4¼″, plus seam allowance. The measurements that follow are for making a bag with a name panel this size. You
will have to adjust these dimensions to construct a tote using your own
name if it is longer than the name shown. If your name is shorter or you
wish to use initials, center the letters in the 8″ length described. But no matter how you alter the length of the panel, the width will remain the same. Be
sure to add a ¼″ seam allowance on all sides, whatever the measurements.

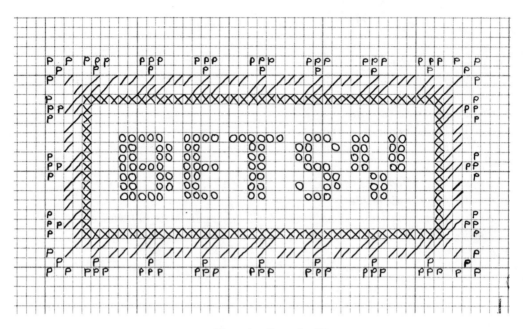

Chart for Sampler Tote.

Color key for Sampler Tote:

Symbol	Color
Y̶	DARK YELLOW
Y	YELLOW
b	BROWN
⊠	DARK GREEN
⧄	LIGHT GREEN
⬤	TURQUOISE
O	BLUE
∩	WHITE
S	SALMON
P	PINK

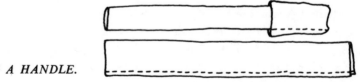

MAKING A HANDLE.

Fold fabric in half lengthwise, right sides together. Stitch. Turn right side out.

Preparation

Press all materials.

Procedure

Step 1

Chart on graph paper the name to be stitched, according to the alphabet on page 19, leaving 16 empty boxes on all sides. Experiment on the graph paper to determine the best letter spacing. Leave at least 2 spaces between the letters at the base. Find and mark on the completed graph the vertical and horizontal center stitches of the name. If the name is not evenly divisible, mark the vertical center off by one stitch.

Step 2

Chart the border around the name. The corner and side stitching will remain the same as that shown in the Betsy chart, but you may have to adjust the top and bottom border lines. To do this, decide how many more (or less) stitches are needed. Divide this number in half and plan to add (or subtract) an equal number of stitches at the center of the border, as shown in the Betsy chart. If only a few more stitches are involved, add (or subtract) them at either side of the central flower motif, as shown on page 23. If many stitches are needed, add portions or entire flower motifs to each side of the central flower. Add equal stitches to each side. If, however, you need an uneven number of stitches for your design, first add an extra stitch to the central flower and then position equal amounts of stitches on both sides. The border placement begins 6 stitches outside the name stitchery on all sides, as shown in the accompanying chart. For ease in centering an uneven name, place your border 7 stitches from name and adjust the side borders by adding an extra green stitch on each side of the central side motif, as shown on page 23.

Step 3

Complete stitchery according to the chart you have planned, using the colors in the materials list. When making cross-stitches, cover 2 threads at a time. An embroidery hoop will make your work easier.

Step 4

When cross-stitching is complete, press work lightly on back and prepare materials for patchwork, as given in the materials list. Adjust any measurements as suggested.

Step 5

Add shorter beige strips to top and bottom of stitched name panel, as shown. Pin fabric strips, one at a time, face to face with stitchery and sew in place ¼″ from the outer edge. Open into position, press, and add the longer side strips, using the same technique.

Step 6

Add the outer green borders, using the same technique. When stitching is complete, open and press again.

Step 7

Lay two 25″×1½″ strips on top of each other and construct a handle by folding and pinning them together lengthwise, right sides facing in. Machine-stitch down one side. Remove pins and turn right side out by gently pulling fabric through opening at one end of the tube, as shown. Press flat. Construct a second handle, using the same method.

SAMPLER TOTE CONSTRUCTION:

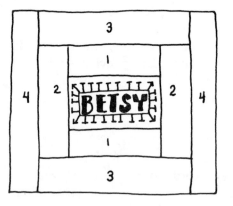

1. Adding patchwork borders.

Step 8

Construct the tote front by pinning completed patchwork panel face to face
with beige lining panel. Be sure handle is pinned between the 2 layers, as
shown. Stitch around the 4 sides, leaving a 3″ opening on the bottom edge
for reversing the fabric. When the stitching is complete, clip the corners on
the diagonal, reverse to right side out, and press. Be sure to turn in the
open seam and hand-stitch it closed.

Step 9

Construct the tote back, using the same method. Again, pin handle in position. Reverse and press.

Step 10

Place the completed front and back face to face. Pin securely and machine-
stitch down the sides and across the bottom. Remove pins, clip corners, and
turn right side out.

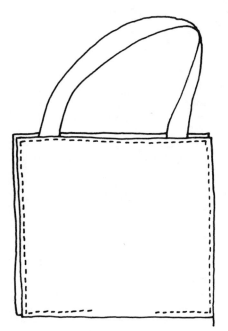

2. Sandwiching handle between
front panel and lining.

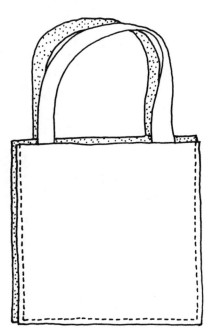

3. Assembling the bag by stitching
completed front and back panels
together face to face.

GINGHAM SAMPLER QUILT.

 cross-stitched gingham *quilted hearts* *rickrack and lace trimming*

GINGHAM SAMPLER QUILT

Finished size: 72″×98¾″

Betsy Potter is a devoted needleworker who always likes to have a project in progress. When she discovered what fun it was to cross-stitch on gingham, she began decorating square patches with geometric borders. Although she had no thoughts about the end product, inspiration came as the piles grew. Betsy decided to make a bedspread for her daughter Liza, who was then just an infant. Today Liza is big enough to sleep in a bed, and she's lucky enough to sleep in the bed once slept in by her great-grandmother, under a quilt made by her mother!

Materials Needed

For central checkerboard panel:
39 gingham rectangles, approximately 8 boxes per inch, each 6″×6¼″, plus seam allowance, in assorted pale colors such as gray-blue, turquoise, pink, orange, violet, green
38 white cotton-blend rectangles, each 6″×6¼″, plus seam allowance.

For inner patchwork border:
2 strips white cotton-blend fabric, each 9″×56″, plus seam allowance
2 strips white cotton-blend fabric, each 7″×68¾″, plus seam allowance

For outer patchwork border and quilt backing:
1 pale yellow cotton-blend sheet at least 88″×110¾″

For quilt filling:
Quilt batting or thin flannel, 72″×98¾″

For trim on inner border:
57 yards medium yellow rickrack (for 2 rows)

For trim on outer border:
75 yards medium white rickrack (for 2 rows)
38 yards white lace

For the centers of each gingham square (optional):
39 commercial flower appliqués

For cross-stitch on gingham:
6-strand embroidery floss in the same colors as gingham but in darker shades

Cardboard template cut to the shape of a heart
Pencil
Ruler
Straight pins

Basting thread
Embroidery needle
Quilting needle
Scissors
Sewing machine
White thread for machine
Yellow thread for machine
White quilting thread
Quilting hoop or frame
Embroidery hoop

Unusual Characteristics

Because Betsy didn't decide on the checkerboard pattern until the gingham cross-stitched rectangles were complete, there is no discernible repeat color pattern within the quilt top. You can make your quilt symmetrical, if you wish, by planning the color placement on paper before you cut and embroider the rectangles.

Since this was an improvised project, you will find other inconsistencies as well. The problem, again, is caused by the gingham. Each color that Betsy used had a slightly different number of boxes per inch, and the boxes themselves are not square. Betsy worked to accommodate the materials as best she could, and you will have to also as you choose gingham in the shades you like.

Accept these qualities as part of the personal aspect of needlework. The finished quilt is so durable and has such strong visual appeal that no one else will notice the irregular border motifs.

Procedure: Quilt Top

Step 1

Plan color placement of gingham rectangles on paper (optional).

Step 2

Trace the required number of 6″×6¼″ rectangles onto the face of both gingham and white fabrics, using cardboard template and pencil or dressmaker's chalk. Leave at least ½″ between rectangles. (See materials list and your own color plan if you have made one.)

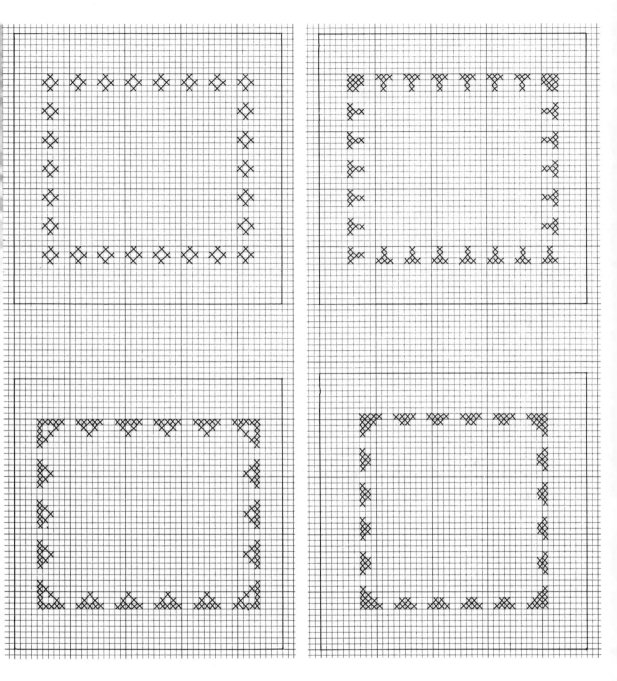

Patterns for Gingham Sampler Quilt (part 1).

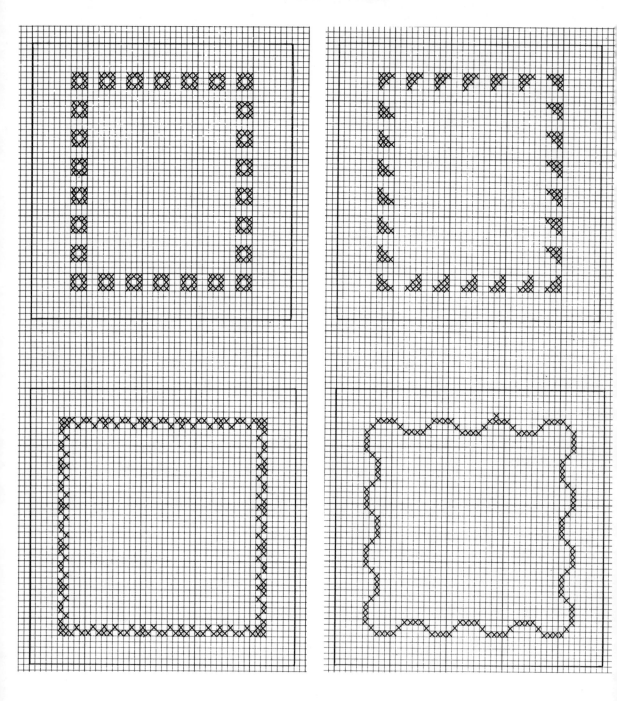

Step 3

Cut out all gingham and white rectangles, leaving ¼″ seam allowance on all sides.

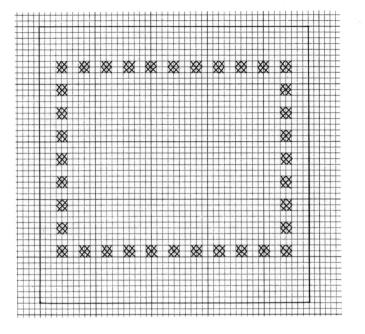

Patterns for Gingham Sampler Quilt (part 2).

Step 4

Embroider cross-stitch motifs on gingham rectangles, using 2 strands of embroidery floss. Select patterns from those shown in this section. Use a small embroidery hoop. When cross-stitching is complete, add optional appliqué flowers to the center of each motif, if desired.

Step 5: Assembling the Patchwork Quilt Top

When embroidery is complete, press all materials. Lay out all rectangles, face up, in checkerboard pattern. Use the floor if necessary.

Step 6

Withdraw 2 adjoining rectangles from the first horizontal row in layout. Placing them face to face, hold them up to a bright window or light to align the drawn seam lines along the 6¼″ side. Place 3 straight pins perpendicular to the drawn line to secure the rectangles together, if necessary, as shown.

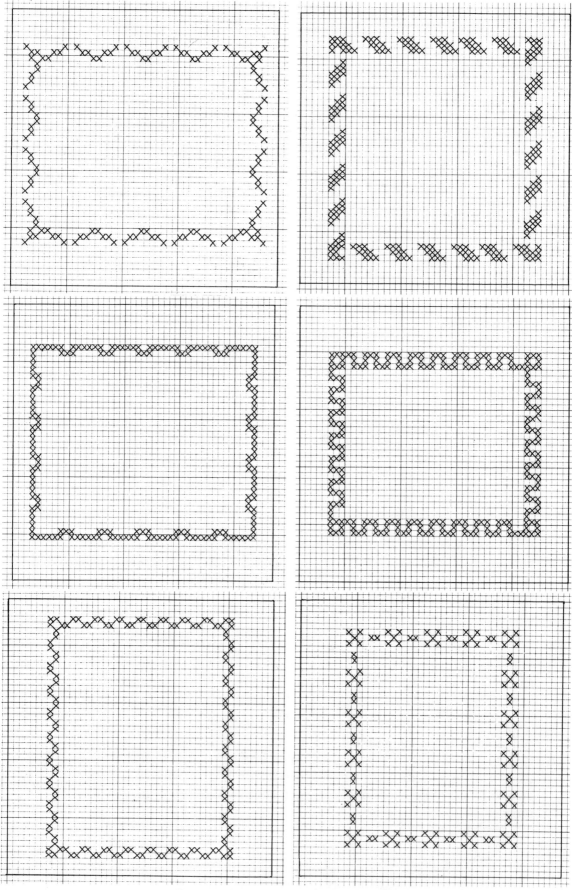

Patterns for Gingham Sampler Quilt (part 3).

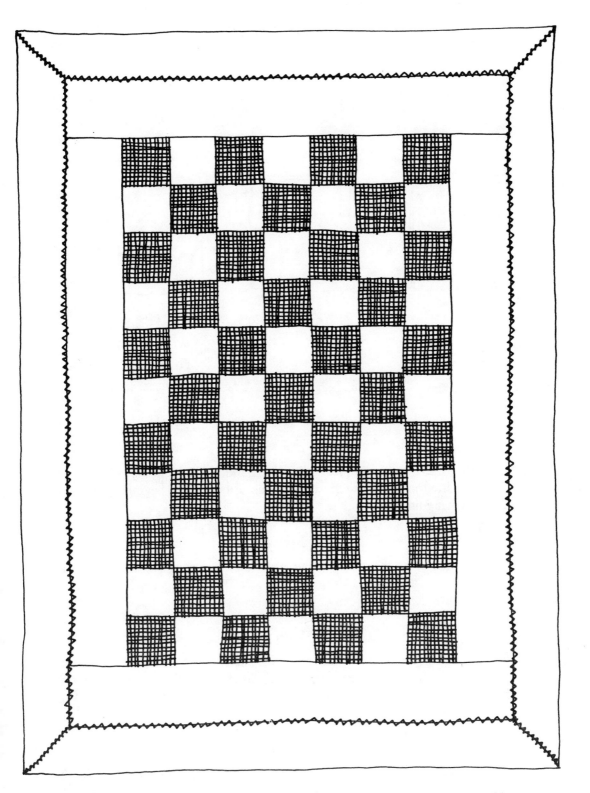

Basic fabric placement for Gingham Sampler Quilt, with machine zigzag stitching (optional). Add quilted hearts before doing final construction; they are omitted here for clarity.

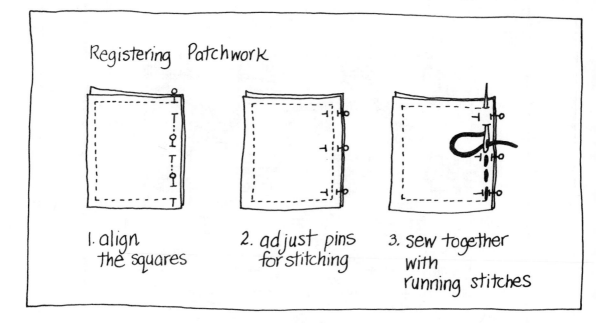

Registering Patchwork

1. align the squares

2. adjust pins for stitching

3. sew together with running stitches

Step 7

Sew along the appropriate seam line by hand (with running stitches) or with a medium machine stitch. Take a backstitch at the beginning and end of each sewing line.

Step 8

Remove pins. Press the stitched pair open on the wrong side of the fabric, with both seam allowances sitting to one side. Place the pair, face up, back in the layout.

Step 9

Join all possible pairs, using this method. Then sew the pairs together, face to face, to form strips. Since you will be working with an odd number of increments, you will not always be able to work with pairs. Attach the single units as needed.

Step 10

Press fabric open after each stitching. Do not pull tightly against the stitches, as this will weaken the seams. If the stitching is visible, the seams are being strained.

Step 11

Join all strips together, 2 at a time, using the method described above. Align all of the strips with pins before doing final sewing.

Step 12

Remove pins. Press completed 42″×68¾″ patchwork panel.

Step 13

Add next the inner white patchwork borders, using the same method. Press.

Joining a row of rectangles into a patchwork strip.

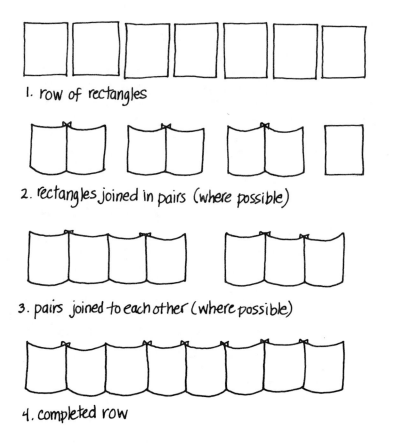

1. row of rectangles

2. rectangles joined in pairs (where possible)

3. pairs joined to each other (where possible)

4. completed row

Step 14

Trace the heart template in position in each white rectangle and along the white patchwork borders, as shown.

The quilt top is now complete.

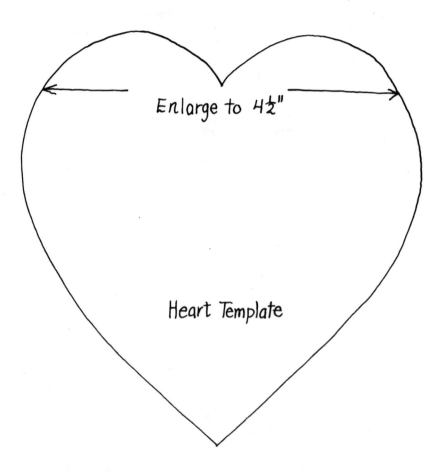

Enlarge to 4½"

Heart Template

Procedure: Quilt Construction

Step 1

Press all materials except quilt batting.

Step 2

Lay out the quilt backing face down on a large, clear, hard, flat surface. Use the floor, if necessary.

Step 3

Center the quilt filling over the backing. Tape down the edges, if necessary, to prevent shifting.

Step 4

Place the completed patchwork top face up on the quilt filling. Use the side of your hand to smooth away any bulges.

Step 5

Pin and baste the 3 layers together, working from the center of the quilt outward to avoid buckling. Baste each white rectangle to be quilted with a separate large crisscross.

Step 6

Trim the quilt filling so that there are 8 inches sticking out from under the quilt top along the sides and 6 inches along the top and bottom. The quilt backing should stick out 8 inches along the sides and 6 inches along the top and bottom *beyond* this.

Step 7

Hand-quilt each heart, as described on page 50. Use a quilting hoop or frame. Again, work from the center out. Remove basting as it gets in the way.

Step 8

When all the hearts are quilted, pin 2 rows of yellow rickrack trim on the white border. Machine-stitch in place. Remove the pins.

Step 9

Lay the quilt out on a flat surface, face up. Fold the yellow backing fabric around to the front of the quilt and fold it over the batting so there is a ¼″ hem overlapping the white patchwork border. Press edge of quilt and hem. Pin securely. (DO NOT press quilting.) Miter and pin corners, as shown.

Step 10

Machine-stitch hem and corners. Remove pins. Press. The quilt construction is now complete.

Step 11

Pin an additional 3 rows of white trim, as described in the materials list, along the yellow border. Machine-stitch in place.

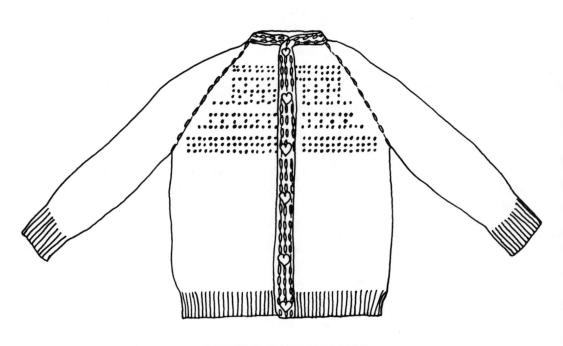

SAMPLER BABY SWEATER.

SAMPLER BABY SWEATER

Use cross-stitch on a sweater to create a unique personalized effect. Add pink and blue heart buttons for a finished look. This project may look forbiddingly complicated, but once you have mastered the simple cross-stitch you'll be delighted with how easy it is to cover the sweater with whimsical patterns. If you are a knitter, make your own basic cardigan with a standard knit-purl ("stockinette") surface. If not, use a sweater you already own or buy one to decorate. The sweater shown was knitted by my grandmother for her first great-grandchild. I embroidered it with brightly colored stitches in just a few sittings.

To decorate your own, follow the patterns on the chart, lengthening or shortening the lines of pattern as needed, according to the size of your sweater. Use good-quality embroidery floss, or do as I did and use Persian yarn left over from needlepoint projects.

Materials Needed

Simple white cardigan baby sweater with raglan sleeves knitted on size 3 or
  4 needles, according to the size of the wool
Persian yarn, ¼ ounce of each of the following colors:
  blue
  turquoise
  pink
  yellow
  light green
  dark green
Tapestry needle
Scissors

Unusual Characteristics

Although the sweater used for this project is a baby sweater, you may also
choose a larger, heavier knit sweater to decorate. Use 2, 3, or 4 strands of
Persian yarn for the embroidery, but experiment first to test for color-
fastness and to find the best weight before you proceed with the decoration.

Preparation

Wash and block sweater, if needed.

Procedure

Step 1

On one side of the sweater, count the stitches from the shoulder seam to the
buttonhole placket just below the neckband in the location you intend to
make the first row of embroidery. Compare this count with that shown on
the accompanying chart and plan to add or subtract stitches to fit your
needs.

Step 2

With 2 strands of blue Persian yarn in a tapestry needle, put in the top row of cross-stitch embroidery on the front of one side of the cardigan sweater, as shown on the chart.

Step 3

When the row is complete, end off, and embroider row 2 in turquoise.

Step 4

Row 3 is left blank, so skip to row 4 and put in pink stitching.

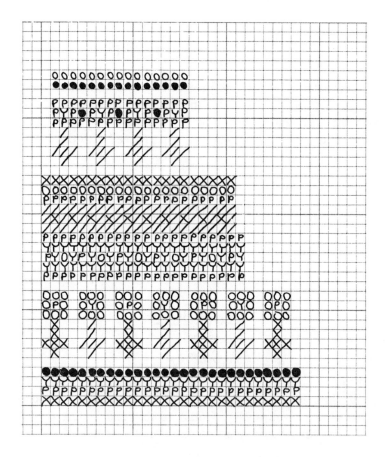

Chart for Sampler Baby Sweater.

Step 5

In row 5, embroider every other stitch with pink yarn, as shown on the chart. When this is complete, add yellow stitching as shown, and then turquoise. Then stitch another row of pink.

Cross-stitch on a knit surface.

Step 6

Put in light green stitching in vertical rows, as shown.

Step 7

Continue to follow the chart as described above, making any necessary adjustments to fit your sweater.

Step 8

Use the running stitch to weave pink and green lines into the front placket, neckband, and raglan shoulder seams.

Color key for Sampler Baby Sweater:

▼	DARK YELLOW
⊻	YELLOW
ⓑ	BROWN
⊠	DARK GREEN
⧄	LIGHT GREEN
◉	TURQUOISE
⊙	BLUE
⋒	WHITE
⑤	SALMON
ⓟ	PINK

SAMPLER BABY BIB.

SAMPLER BABY BIB

Finished size approximately 8½″×10″

The embroidered baby bib is an ideal gift for a special new person—it's comfortable for a baby to wear and fun to look at. Parents will need to be assured that it can be tossed into the washer and dryer for easy laundering. It hardly matters if there's no time for ironing, because even if the bib is slightly rumpled, the baby will prefer it to a stiff plastic bib.

This is such a quick, fun gift project that you might want to make two bibs. Consider making a second in light blue gingham with bright red, yellow, and green stitching.

Materials Needed

Green gingham, 7 squares to the inch, 10″×12″
Lightweight white terry cloth, 10″×12″
29″ jumbo green rickrack
40″ green bias tape
6-strand embroidery floss, 1 skein of each of the following colors:
   bright yellow
   bright blue
   bright red
   light green
   white
   brown
Green sewing thread
Embroidery needle
Scissors
Sewing machine
Embroidery hoop
Straight pins
Basting thread
Pencil or chalk

Unusual Characteristics

The size of gingham checks varies from fabric to fabric. If gingham with 7 squares to the inch is not available, choose gingham in the next closest size. Use the directions that follow to complete your bib, but be prepared for slightly different results. Gingham with larger boxes (and fewer squares per inch) will have bolder cross-stitches which may need to be worked with 4 strands of floss. Smaller, more delicate gingham may need only 2 strands. Experiment to find the best effect before beginning final stitching.

Preparation

Iron all fabrics as needed.

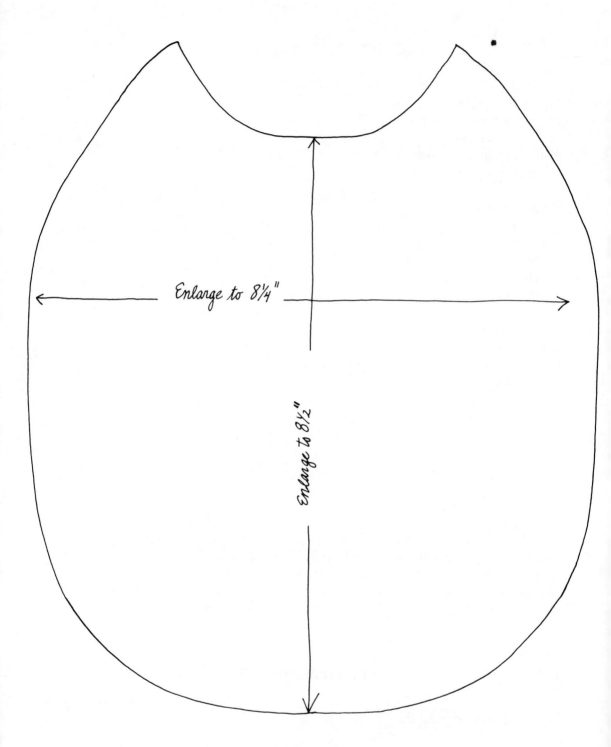

Enlarge to 8¼"

Enlarge to 8½"

Outline of bib.

Procedure

Step 1

Enlarge the outline of the bib to 8¼″ wide by 8½″ long, as shown in the drawing.

Cut out shape and trace onto gingham and terry cloth, using pencil or chalk.

Step 2

Stitch long basting lines through the outline of the bib on both gingham and terry cloth.

Step 3

Mark the horizontal and vertical centers of the gingham fabric with 2 basting lines.

Chart and color key for Sampler Baby Bib:

BRIGHT YELLOW: A, *bird outline, and cat's eyes*
BRIGHT BLUE: B *and cat outline*
BRIGHT RED: C, *apple outline, bird's eyes and beak, and cat's nose*
WHITE: *bird's wings and cat's whiskers and paws*
BROWN: *apple stem and bird's legs*
LIGHT GREEN: *apple leaves*

Step 4

Using the bib chart, stitch the letters using 3 strands of embroidery floss. Make one complete cross-stitch per box. Use an embroidery hoop. Carefully remove any *interior* basting lines as they get in the way.

Step 5

Embroider the apple, bird, and cat, using backstitches, as shown on page 35. Place them along or through each gingham square as shown. The bird's eye and the cat's eye and nose are french knots, illustrated on page 37.

Step 6

When the stitching is complete, remove any remaining interior basting lines and trim away excess fabric, leaving ¼" seam allowance on all sides. Press fabric again. Baste jumbo rickrack around the outside edge of the bib on the right side. Center the rickrack over the outline basting.

Step 7

Pin bib with rickrack face to face with the terry cloth. Machine-stitch around the outside edges, making sure to catch the rickrack in the sewing line. Do *not* stitch across the top of the bib.

Step 8

When the stitching is complete, remove the pins and remaining basting lines. Turn the bib right side out and press.

Step 9

Lay out the length of bias tape on a flat surface and center the bib on it. Fold the tape in half, widthwise, so the bib is firmly caught between the layers.

Step 10

Baste the entire length of bias tape, doubled over, making sure the bib is firmly caught between the layers.

Step 11

Beginning at one end, machine-stitch the entire length of tape in place. When the stitching is complete, remove the pins. For durability, check again to see that the bib is securely fastened between the layers of tape. If not, carefully remove stitching and attach again.

KNIT BABY OVERALLS

The baby overalls were knitted by Connie Washburne as a gift for my son Jesse. Using a pattern book from about 1950 for directions, she chose an up-to-date acrylic yarn to create durable and washable shorts. Adapting the bib design from another knitted garment shown in the same book, Connie used 6-strand cotton embroidery floss and a blunt tapestry needle to work continental stitches into the knit surface of the overalls bib.

If you are a knitter, look for an appropriate pattern among today's pattern books, or look through old magazines in the library or at a used-book store.

As a variation, use removable scrim canvas (see page 81) to cross-stitch the sailboat design on the bib of simple corduroy or cotton overalls.

Materials Needed

Simple knitted overalls with rectangular or square bib
Tapestry needle
Scissors
6-strand cotton embroidery floss, 1 skein of each of the following colors:
  red
  white
  green
  yellow

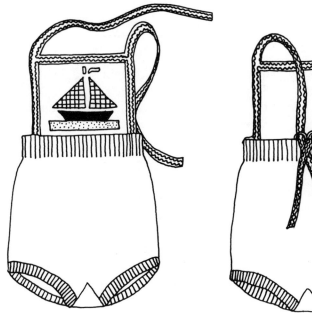

KNIT BABY OVERALLS.

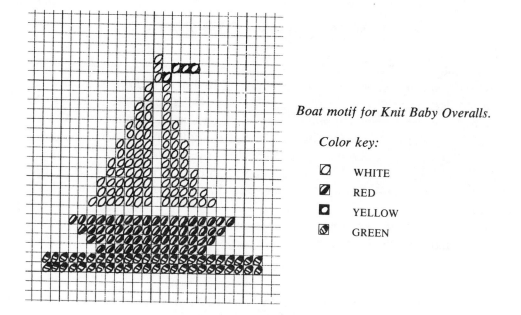

Boat motif for Knit Baby Overalls.

Color key:

☑   WHITE

☑   RED

☑   YELLOW

☑   GREEN

Preparation

Count the knitted stitches of the bib and place basting stitches for centering through the horizontal and vertical centers of the areas to be embroidered.

Procedure

Using the accompanying sailboat chart, begin stitching in the center of the design. Either use 3 strands of the 6-strand floss with the continental stitch or cross-stitch with 2 strands of floss. Keep the stitching loose to avoid distorting knitted surface.

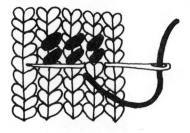

Continental stitch on a knit surface.

NEEDLEPOINT SAMPLER BELT

Finished size: 1¼"×36"

This dynamic needlepoint belt will add a touch of elegance to any outfit. Made by Dorothy Twining Globus, who delights in improvising with geometric patterns, each square has its own special jewel-like image. Many of Dorothy's patterns are given below, but once you copy one or two, you will probably find yourself devising patterns of your own. Dorothy bought yarn in colors that appealed to her, and you may wish to choose colors of your own to create a belt to blend with your own tastes and wardrobe.

Materials Needed

Mono mesh, 14 threads to the inch, 1¼"×36", plus ample seam allowance on all sides, edges taped

Persian yarn, ½ ounce each of assorted colors such as those shown on the chart

Tapestry needle

Scissors

Graph paper and pencil

Waterproof marker

Belt buckle in plastic, metal, wood, in an appropriate color, with a 1½" central shaft (available in yard goods shops)

Grosgrain ribbon, 1¼" by 37" (for belt back)

Sewing needle and thread

Straight pins

NEEDLEPOINT SAMPLER BELT

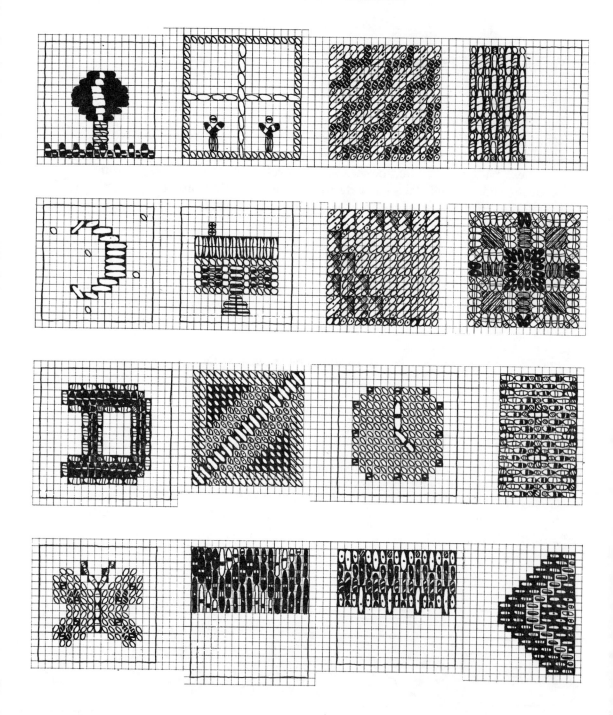

MOTIFS FOR NEEDLEPOINT SAMPLER BELT.

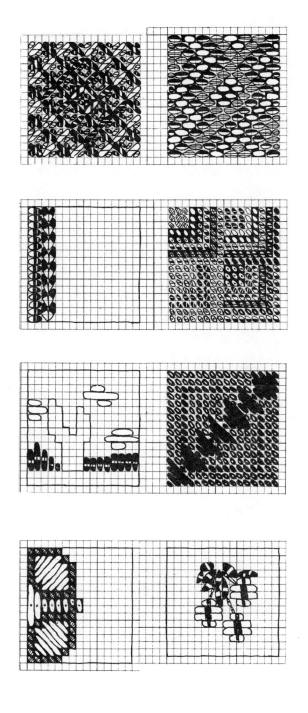

Color key for Needlepoint Sampler Belt:

⊘	⊞	AQUA
⊘	⊞	DARK AQUA
◓	⊟	YELLOW
◓	⊕	ORANGE
⊘	⊞	OCHER
◓	⊞	DARK OCHER
◔	⊟	WHITE
◓	⊜	DARK GREEN
◓	◉	MEDIUM GREEN
◓	⊜	LIGHT GREEN (APPLE)
◔	⊞	GRAY-GREEN
◔	⊕	ORANGE
◔	⊞	RED
◔	⊟	PINK
⊕	⊟	RUST
◼	⊟	BROWN
◼	⬤	SALMON
◓	⊞	BLUE
◼	⊞	NAVY BLUE
◼	⊞	INDIGO
◼	⬤	GRAY
◓	◑	VIOLET
◓	⊞	DARK VIOLET
◓	⊞	LAVENDER
◓	⊞	DARK BROWN

Indicates continental stitch

Indicates straight stitch over 2 threads

Preparation

Using a waterproof marker, outline the belt shape on the mesh. Cut the needlepoint mesh to size, leaving ample seam allowance on all sides. Bind the raw edges with masking tape.

Procedure

Step 1

Starting at the right-hand end of the belt, put in one complete design chosen from the accompanying charts. Use 2 strands of needlepoint yarn in your needle to make a combination of continental and bargello stitches, as needed. Be sure to leave a generous seam allowance to the right of the stitching to use later when attaching the belt buckle.

Step 2

When the first pattern is complete, put in a single vertical line along the left side of the motif to define the edge. Use the continental stitch and a dark color wool.

Step 3

Put in another needlepoint motif. When it is complete, add a single vertical line in the same dark color as before along the left side to define the edge.

Step 4

Continue to add patterns and to define each finished square with a vertical line. This will create a grid-like appearance. Each motif will be approximately 15 by 15 stitches, plus a dividing line on each side. If you are improvising, you may find yourself creating patterns with widths that contain slightly different stitch counts. This is acceptable.

Step 5

When you reach the desired length, add a pointed design to end the belt, such as the bargello motif shown on the chart.

Finishing

You can finish this belt at home according to the following instructions or have the work done at a reliable needlework shop.

Blocking

Block the belt according to instructions on page 42. Trim all seam allowances to ½″.

Belt Construction

Turn the top and bottom seam allowances to the back of the belt.

At one end, turn under the seam allowance and miter (see page 50) to define the pointed end of the belt. Do not fold over the opposite end, which is to be fastened to the belt buckle, as this will add undesirable bulk.

Using yarn in the same color as the dividing lines in the belt, make whip stitches to bind the top and bottom edges of the belt, as shown in drawing A. Make one stitch per box of mesh.

Slip the belt through the buckle, shown in B.

Wrap 1¼″ of the unfinished end of the belt over the center shaft of the belt buckle. Attach the belt to itself on the back with small stitches, as shown in C.

Using small stitches and a hand sewing needle and thread, sew grosgrain ribbon over the back to finish the belt, as shown in D.

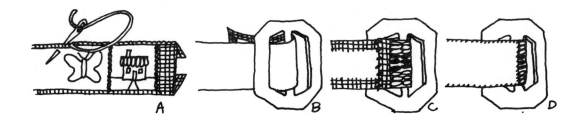

Adding a buckle to the Needlepoint Sampler Belt.

STENCIL ALPHABET PILLOW (INCLUDING PATCHWORK BORDERS).

STENCIL ALPHABET PILLOW

Finished size: 16½″×14½″

A fast, easy project with the look of a traditional sampler, this pillow was made with stencils and permanent felt-tipped markers. For the strongest effect, keep all of your colors and materials simple, and choose ribbon trim that is a solid color or is woven with a primitive, color enhancing design.

Materials Needed

1 piece muslin, 10½″×8½″, plus seam allowance
2 pieces gingham, each 3″×10½″, plus seam allowance
2 pieces gingham, each 3″×14½″, plus seam allowance
2 pieces printed ribbon, each 16½″×½″, plus seam allowance at ends
2 pieces printed ribbon, each 14½″×½″, plus seam allowance at ends
Fabric for pillow back, 14½″×16½″, plus seam allowance
2 pieces muslin, each 14½″×16½″, plus seam allowance, for pillow lining (optional)
Precut plastic stencil sheets with ½″ roman letters and numbers (※14 E-Z Letter Quik Stik [P.O. Box 829, 42 Locust Street, Westminster, Md. 21157] is available in many stationery, variety, and art supply stores)
Translucent stencil paper or 2-ply acetate, 8½″×10½″
Small swivel-blade utility knife with sharp edge
Fine-line felt-tip markers with permanent ink, in the following colors:
    forest green
    blue
    scarlet
    dark yellow
Pencil
Masking tape
Iron
Cardboard or pile of newspaper for cutting surface
Straight pins
Dacron polyester fiberfill, 12-ounce bag
Sewing machine

Procedure

Step 1

Enlarge and trace stencil house, trees, rabbits, and border outline onto stencil paper or acetate.

Step 2

Using a swivel-blade knife, cut out stencil. Be sure work surface is well protected.

Step 3

Iron muslin and tape securely to a smooth, flat surface.

Step 4

Test each marker on a scrap of muslin before applying to stencil. Most new markers will bleed uncontrollably on fabric. Although a small amount of bleeding is normal, to minimize excess bleeding, let markers sit uncovered in a well-ventilated room for several minutes before testing again. Each color will respond differently. It is better to build up colors slowly on your fabric with pens that are too dry rather than work with a pen that is too moist.

Step 5

Center the border stencil on the muslin and tape securely in place. Using markers, slowly and carefully fill in each area of the stencil, as indicated in the drawing. The tiny flowers on each side of the house are drawn freehand, as shown in the accompanying illustration.

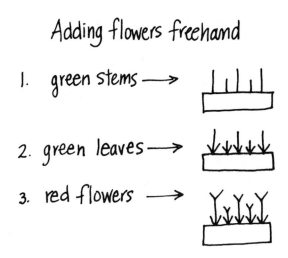

ADDING PATCHWORK BORDERS.

1. *Pin fabric strip across the bottom edge face to face with the sampler.*

2. *Stitch in position.*

3. *When top and bottom strips are sewn in place, press open. Pin and stitch side strips in position, face to face with sampler.*

4. *Open and press patchwork strips in final position. To add an additional border in a contrasting color, use the same technique.*

Step 6

When the border is complete, remove the stencil. Center the plastic alphabet stencil in position and tape securely. Be sure all plastic is punched out of stencil. You may need a small pointed tool, such as a tapestry needle, to do this.

Step 7

Using alternating red, yellow, and blue, fill in the letters with felt-tip markers, as previously described. Fill in the letters as they are spaced on the stencil sheet.

Step 8

When the alphabet is complete, remove the stencil. On a scrap of paper, mark out your name, the date, and your location using tighter spacing. Using the alphabet stencil again, keep your letters close but do not let them touch. Abbreviate information, if needed.

Step 9

When you have established appropriate spacing, stencil this information in position on the sampler. For clarity, stencil your name, date, and location each in a different color.

Step 10 (Optional)

If your plastic stencil sheet is 8″×10″, center and tape it over your completed design and trace around the outside edge with a fine red marker to establish a border outline. You may also consider using a pencil and ruler to draw an outline that you can trace over with a red marker.

Step 11

Iron the completed stenciled design.

Special Note: *Whether you begin by adding patchwork borders to the top and bottom of your sampler, or to the sides, the technique is the same. Be sure that the first panels you add are the same length as the corresponding edges of the sampler (plus seam allowance).*

1. Pin ribbons along top and bottom panels. Machine straight stitch along top and bottom edges of ribbon. Remove pins.

Procedure: Patchwork Border Construction

Step 1

Add gingham strips to the top and bottom of the muslin pillow face, as shown in the accompanying illustration.

Step 2

Add gingham strips to each side, using the same technique.

Step 3

Press with a hot iron. Pin ribbon along top and bottom gingham strips, approximately ⅜" from inner edge, as shown. Machine-stitch in place along both edges of ribbon.

Step 4

Remove pins.

Step 5

Pin ribbon on side gingham strips. Machine-stitch in place. Remove pins and press.

2. Pin ribbons along side panels. Stitch as described above.

Procedure: Pillow Construction

Step 1

Pin completed pillow top face to face with fabric back. For a stronger pillow, pin optional muslin lining pieces, one on top of each side.

Step 2

Beginning on the bottom, machine-stitch around all 4 sides, ¼" from outer edge, leaving a 4" opening at the center of the bottom for reversing the pillow.

Step 3

Clip corners on the diagonal, ⅛" from stitching. Remove all pins. Turn pillow right side out and stuff with Dacron polyester fiberfill.

Step 4

Pin and hand-stitch closed.

STENCIL BIRTHDAY PILLOW.

STENCIL BIRTHDAY PILLOW

Finished size: 12¾"×20"

For a unique birthday sampler pillow that you can make in an evening, stencil a personal message on muslin using ready-made stencil letters. Choose materials to match the environment of the lucky recipient. A simple border fabric will suggest an open, contemporary feeling, but for a stencil sampler with a more historic look choose delicate floral fabric instead. Consider adding several patchwork borders around your message and perhaps a ruffle, as shown in the Grandma Pillow on page 107.

Materials Needed

1 piece muslin, 15"×7¾" (or lengthen for longer name), plus seam allowance

2 pieces gingham, each 15" (or longer, to match muslin)×2½", plus seam allowance

2 pieces gingham, each 12¾"×2½", plus seam allowance

Gingham for pillow back, 12¾"×20", plus seam allowance

2 pieces muslin, each 12¾"×20", plus seam allowance, for pillow lining (optional)

Precut plastic stencil sheets with 1½" gothic capitals and numbers (⚹33 E-Z Letter Quik Stik, see page 157) and ½" gothic letters (⚹14 E-Z Letter Quik Stik)

Fine-line felt-tip markers with permanent ink, in blue, red, and green

Pencil

Paper, 15"×7¾"

Scissors

Straight pins

Dacron polyester fiberfill, 16-ounce bag

Sewing machine

Iron

(Note:) *This drawing shows position of words only. To make this pillow, use precut plastic stencil letters sheets described in materials list. Purchasing information is given on page 4.*

Color key:

BLUE: *"Happy Birthday," name of giver(s)*
RED: *name of recipient, "love"*
GREEN: *date and small alphabet*

Procedure

Step 1

On paper, using a pencil and the stencil sheets, mark out your message to establish placement. Keep letters close together but not touching. For the alphabet on the side, use the loose, predetermined spacing of the stencil sheets.

Step 2

Iron muslin. Tape the completed stencil message on a hard, flat surface. Smooth out and tape the muslin over this.

Step 3

Test each marker on a scrap of muslin before applying to final surface, as described in Step 4 of the Stencil Alphabet Pillow on page 159.

Step 4

Using the drawing underneath as a placement guide, begin to fill in the letters of the birthday message. Hold the stencil firmly in place as you work, and reposition after each letter is complete. Work slowly, touching markers lightly to the fabric. Dry markers are easier to control than those which are fresh and moist.

Step 5

When the birthday message is complete, use the smaller letters to sign the pillow on the left side, as shown. Use this same sheet to stencil the alphabet.

Step 6

When stenciling is complete, iron the muslin again and add the gingham borders, as shown on page 160. Sew top and bottom borders first.

Step 7

Complete pillow construction, as described on page 45.

The enclosed areas show word placement. Use precut stencil letters described in materials list. Purchasing information is given on page 4.

YELLOW CAT PILLOW

Finished size: 18½"×14¼"

Cat lovers will adore this contemporary sampler cat pillow which is fun and easy to make with waterproof markers and precut stencil letters. You can either duplicate the serene animal shown or create your own original beast. Whatever your approach, be sure to surround your drawing with your name, location, date, and an alphabet for a rich sampler look.

Enlarge to 12½"

Materials Needed

1 piece muslin, 12½"×8¼", plus seam allowance

2 pieces muslin, each 18½"×14¼", plus seam allowance, for stronger pillow construction (optional)

2 pieces cotton-blend fabric with flowered print, each 3"×12½", plus seam allowance

2 pieces cotton-blend fabric with flowered print, each 3"×18½", plus seam allowance

1 piece cotton-blend fabric with flowered print, 18½"×14¼", plus seam allowance, for pillow back

Precut plastic stencil sheet with ½" roman letters and numbers (※14 E-Z Letter Quik Stik; see page 157)

Fine-line felt-tip markers with permanent ink, in the following colors:
dark yellow
blue
red
green
black

Masking tape

White paper, 12½"×8¼"

Pencil

Ruler

Straight pins

Sewing machine

Iron

Dacron polyester fiberfill, 16-ounce bag

Hand-sewing needle

Thread

Scissors

Procedure

Step 1

On white paper, enlarge the cat drawing to the size indicated, including the outlines of the word-placement areas shown in the first drawing. When the enlargement is complete, darken the lines with a marker to increase visibility.

YELLOW CAT PILLOW.

Step 2

Tape the enlargement to a sunny window or a light table. Smooth muslin over this and tape securely. Using a black fine-line marker with permanent ink, trace the outline of the cat onto the muslin. Touch the pen very lightly to the fabric as you work to prevent excess ink bleeding. For specifics on drawing with permanent markers on muslin, see Step 4 of the Stencil Alphabet Pillow, on page 159.

Step 3

When outlining is complete, remove muslin and artwork from the window. Continue your work on a hard, well-protected desk. Fill in the colors on the cat. The main color is yellow. All others are indicated in the drawing. Again, apply color lightly to fabric. Use many short strokes to create the effect of yellow striped fur. Follow the directional lines shown in the first drawing.

Step 4

When the cat is complete, apply the stencil letters. Place the enlargement drawing under the muslin and use the outlines of the word-placement areas to gauge your stenciling. Slight variation will not alter the overall effect. For a soft look, as shown in the photograph, only outline the letters—do not fill them in.

Procedure: Patchwork Border Construction

Step 1

Add flowered fabric strips to the top and bottom edges of the muslin pillow face, as shown on page 160.

Step 2

Add flowered fabric to the sides, using the same technique.

Step 3

Complete pillow as described on page 45.